AF597286

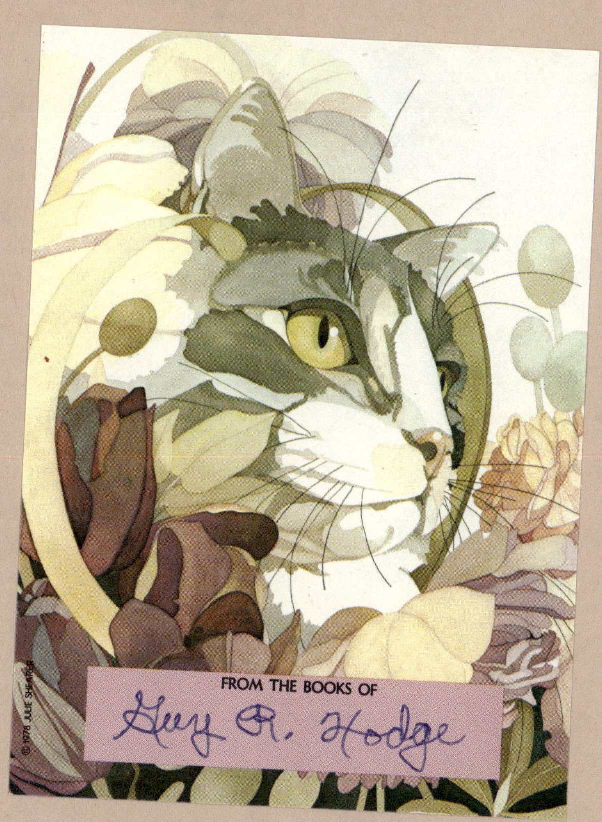
FROM THE BOOKS OF
Guy R. Hodge

Photographs of the American Wilderness

Dean Brown

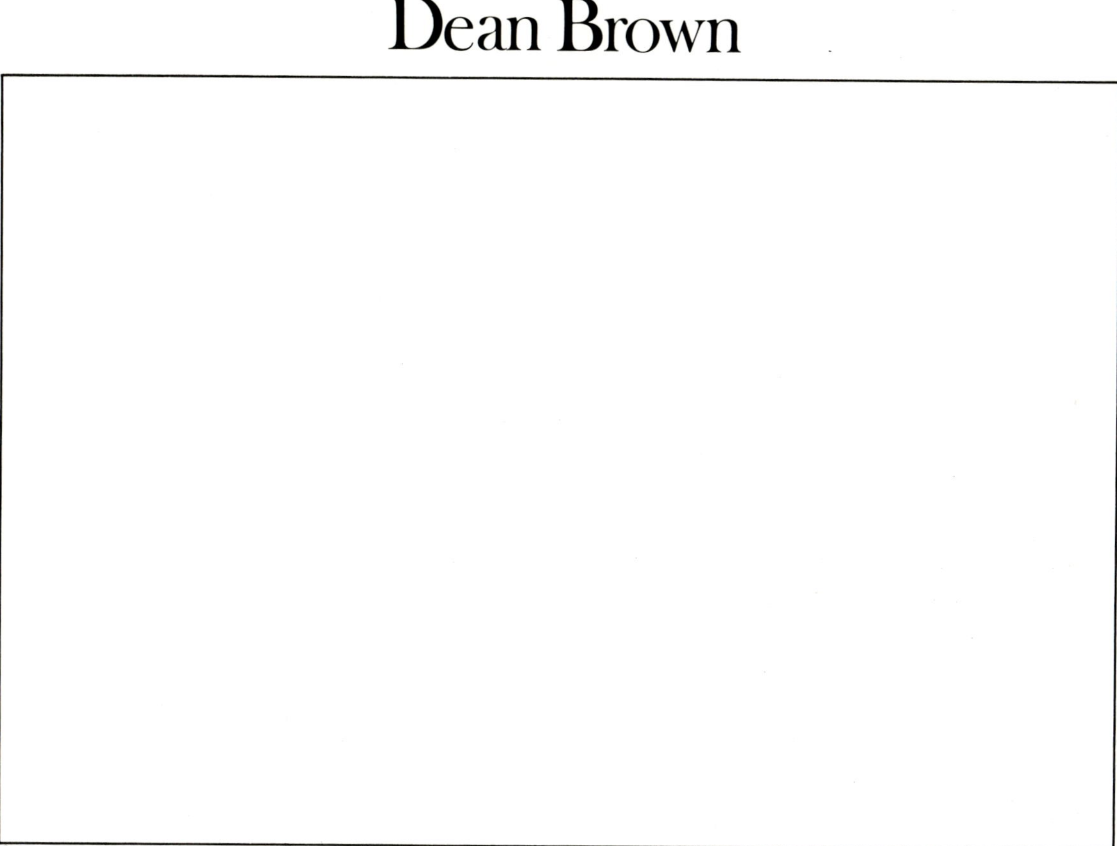

Introduction by Carol Brown

AMPHOTO
American Photographic Book Publishing Co., Inc.
Garden City, New York

The publication of this book was supported by the National Endowment for the Arts, a Federal agency, and by the Dean Brown Fund.

Published by Amphoto for the Akron Art Institute.

Published in Garden City, New York, by
American Photographic Book Publishing Co., Inc.

Library of Congress Catalog Card Number: 76-17423
ISBN: 0-8174-2413-X

Manufactured in the United States of America.

This book was produced in conjunction with a retrospective exhibition of photographs by Dean Brown, which was held at the Akron Art Institute from May 2 through June 13, 1976, and is subsequently being held at the Virginia Museum of Fine Arts, Richmond; Amon Carter Museum of Western Art, Fort Worth, Texas; Witte Memorial Museum, San Antonio, Texas; Krannert Art Museum, University of Illinois, Urbana, Illinois; Indianapolis Museum of Art, Indiana; and other museums and galleries throughout 1977 and 1978. The exhibition was organized for the Akron Art Institute by Carol Brown, Guest Curator. The dye-transfer prints for the show were copied from Dean Brown's original prints where possible and according to Carol Brown's direction; the printing was done at Berkey K and L Custom Labs in New York by Felix Gomes, under the supervision of Ken Lieberman and Fred Horbert.
The book was designed by Bob Ciano.

We would like to express our deepest gratitude to the following institutions and individuals. The support of the National Endowment for the Arts made the show and the book possible. Without its aid, Dean Brown's work would have been lost to all but a handful of people. The participation of the Virginia Museum of Fine Arts, Amon Carter Museum of Western Art, Witte Memorial Museum, Krannert Art Museum, and the Indianapolis Museum of Art contributed greatly to its success. Bob Ciano gave unstintingly of his ideas, time, faith, and talent from the inception of both projects until their completion. The advice and encouragement of Dr. John Jacobus and Dr. David Mann were of vital importance at innumerable difficult moments. Lee Witkin's loyalty was a sustaining force. The concern and aid given by Mr. and Mrs. R. M. Brown were essential throughout. All the contributors to The Dean Brown Fund helped by showing their belief in Dean's work. Ken Lieberman, Fred Horbert, and Felix Gomes took infinite pains to duplicate Dean's photographs as closely as possible. James Enyeart shared with us his ideas for the show. Permission to reproduce certain photographs was graciously extended by Condé Nast and Time Incorporated. Mr. and Mrs. James J. Anderson, Dan Budnik, Evelyne and Howard Daitz, Mary Margaret Goodrich, Jain Kelly, Mary and Weston Naef, Jane Scholl, Mel Scott, Rochelle Zabarkes, and Mr. and Mrs. Louis S. Myers provided invaluable assistance and support. Many other friends helped in many ways. Although they cannot all be mentioned here, they are certainly not forgotten.

Carol Brown
Robert Doty, Director, Akron Art Institute

Preface by Robert Doty

The history of photography is an account of actions and reactions, changing values, new ideas, and steadfast traditions. From the introduction of the first successful photographic process to the end of the nineteenth century, the photographer worked with the single task of rendering the object, person, or scene as clearly and directly as the medium would permit. Meanwhile, the painter had found new ways of representing vision, and by the turn of the century, the photographer felt compelled to emulate the painter and strive for a self-awareness in art that denied clarity and tone. A conscious effort was made to reassert the essential elements. Those who sought to use photography as a means of creating intellectual or spiritual images turned to manipulations of process, or devices such as the closeup. But making images of a specific reality, with implicit photographic means, continued to be a major consideration for many photographers. In recent years, theories have been advanced that question the values inherent in both these stands and relegate the whole process to a position close to futility.

The photographs of Dean Brown are clear, concise documents, rendered with exquisite attention to the faithful representation of the subject. The photographs may be viewed quickly and easily, or they may be slowly and deliberately studied—each method will produce its own rewards. There is nothing ephemeral or forced about Dean's images. They simply illuminate an intimate experience with the land and its unique properties and elements. The medium is never allowed to become more important than the subject. Photography is the means of translating experience, and it was Dean's constant respect for the basic properties of the medium that made a significant translation possible.

The traditions of veracity, clarity, and directness in the photographic image are as old as the medium itself. These characteristics were rediscovered by Edward Weston, who wrote in 1928 that his purpose as a photographer was to "present objectively the texture, rhythm, form in nature without subterfuge or evasion in spirit or technique—to record the quintessence of the object or element before my lens. . . . " Dean respected Weston and the concepts that formed his work. Each image that Dean made is depicted in clear, intricate, and beautiful detail, with forms, lines, and patterns precisely arranged within the frame, and the entire picture energized by the light, which so quickly and completely transforms the appearance of the natural world. A consistent regard for clarity, tonal quality, and the infinite variety and nuance of detail and color pervaded Dean's work throughout his career and enabled him to achieve the photographs for which he shall be remembered.

The surviving areas of the American wilderness, the subject that Dean pursued most avidly, are a deceptive motif. They offer boundless pictorial material and yet yield so few photographs of significance. Images of the wilderness are physically difficult to obtain and equally difficult to do well enough to qualify as great pictures. The land offers such vast opportunities that the photographer is faced with a bewildering complexity of choices. Dean had the rare ability to isolate and select places and moments that both portray the true character of a place and retain an aura of universal beauty. All his efforts were devoted to conveying and expanding a visual awareness of the natural world, from the splendor of mountains and plains to the wonder of tiny living plants and animals, recording what he saw in order that others, as well, might see. It was Dean's special triumph to combine the grandeur of the epic image with the transitory but trenchant effects of the atmosphere on the land. As a result, his images impart a deeper feeling for a place, an intimate sense of being there. Dean's photographs intensify the human response to nature, people, and the infinite values of their relationship.

Every artist must face decisions that ultimately will shape the course of his work. For some, these decisions are few and based on purely intellectual considerations. For them, the studio is a lonely place, and the singular encounters are momentous. For others, decisions must be made constantly, especially for those who engage in the ever-shifting patterns and modes of contemporary life. Dean was one of these people. His earlier pursuits—linguistics, music, teaching—were contemplative and retiring. Photography provided a means to be active and creative at all times. When he took up photography professionally, he did not hesitate to join the highly competitive world of free-lance journalism. Landscape photography demanded as much and also fulfilled a sense of adventure. The decisions still had to be made, and the subject was virtually endless. Photography became a quest from which he never wavered. To a sensitive eye and an unreserved quality of vision, he brought personal conviction, courage, and certainty of purpose—all that was essential for a great photographer.

Robert Doty
Director
Akron Art Institute

Introduction by Carol Brown

"I like to photograph a thing or situation as I find it, without rearrangement or interference . . . "

On July 5, 1973, Dean Brown fell from a mountain. He died on July 8, three days before his thirty-seventh birthday. He had been on assignment photographing a waterfall that had just formed as the result of torrential rains of the previous weeks. He fell from Table Mountain in the Kancamangus Highway section of the White Mountains of New Hampshire. He fell seventy-five feet into a frigid, swollen stream in an almost impenetrable forest. Although he had extensive internal and external injuries, he salvaged the exposed film and tried to protect himself. He sent up a flare.

I had gone looking for him without success, not knowing that he had fallen. When I saw the flare, I immediately went to get the rangers. It was dark by then. The rescue team worked until dawn to bring him out of the forest, carrying him at shoulder height as they forded rushing streams, chopping the dense growth to get the stretcher through.

It was eleven-and-a-half hours from the time he fell until he reached the nearest hospital. He was in too deep a state of shock to risk the extra hour it would have taken to get him to Maine Medical Center, which had more life-sustaining equipment. He was lucid. He told the rescuers what his injuries were as far as he knew. In a voice barely audible, he joked with them about his severed foot and apologized for the trouble he was causing. He urged them to make sure they had all the film. He asked me to call some people who were expecting him to do assignments for them to explain that there would be a delay. His only complaint was that he was very cold.

He died courageously and with humility.

It was characteristic. He did not romanticize. His pictures are accurate records of remarkable moments in nature. He wanted to be able to recognize the extraordinary and to capture it clearly, without tricks. That meant taking infinite pains with his craft and many risks with his life, although he never admitted it. He said he was doing his work as best he could. He said, "As with most of my work, I wanted to disappear, and at this I was apparently pretty successful. . . . I never made any attempt to glamorize or romanticize."

I met him at Cornell. He had extraordinary eyes; that was the first thing everyone noticed. They were blue or grey or green, depending on the light. They looked at everything clearly and with curiosity and understanding. He had an athlete's grace of movement and a scholar's passion for truth. He had a whimsical sense of humor that showed itself in puns and in notes written in preexisting or instantaneously fabricated codes. He had, even then, a staggering number of accomplishments, carefully concealed for the most part. He had excelled in math, science, and languages in his academic life. German and Chinese were his specialties then. He later picked up Japanese, Navajo, Eskimo, Dutch, and Italian as necessary. He had been a long-distance runner and a crack marksman. He had built a ham radio and was a whiz at Morse code. He played the piano, the lute, and the banjo, and he sang in college choruses. He sailed. He had been photographing and developing his own pictures since he was ten years old.

His pursuits were basically solitary. He was raised in Hampton, Virginia, the fifth of six boys. Developing pictures in the dark and running miles through the countryside may have been ways to get some peace and quiet. His inventiveness, persistence in the face of difficulties, and love for the outdoors came from his father, a remarkable self-made businessman. His admiration of the arts came from his mother, a charming descendant of John and Priscilla Alden. His decisions to live in New York and to make his living at photography were departures from family traditions.

For many years he tried compromises: linguistics with music and photography on the side; musicology and teaching with performing music and taking photographs on the side. Finally, he decided to stop doing everything else in order to photograph.

He had left Cornell for New York City before he knew how he wanted to spend his life. For a time, he worked in hospital labs, bookstores, and camera shops. Finally, he went back to school to earn his bachelor's degree—cum laude—at Brooklyn College. By 1967, he had received his master's degree in musicology from New York University, had completed the course work towards his Ph.D., was teaching music at Brooklyn College, and was playing the viola da gamba professionally in concert with the Waverly Consort and other Renaissance music groups. In spite of his grueling schedule, he was spending more and more time on photography, for this was the activity that was giving him the most satisfaction.

He was disillusioned with his academic studies because "the kids who thought they were scholars got quickly involved with IBM computing of often silly questions that made impressive sheaves of data and endless tables." His teaching experience was disheartening to him and he decided never to do it again. "I never liked to work for a corporation and of course a college and teaching music, as I was doing, was the same kind of thing, with the same kind of infighting, the same kind of dirty politics, all that kind of thing, no different at all. I couldn't stand working within that framework and I still can't." Performing music meant always interpreting another's ideas. In photography he could do something unique. Once he was convinced of that, the decision was made.

In 1967, his pictures were mainly of people, although he also shot landscapes when he could get away from the city. Instead of taking posed close-up portraits, he made pictures that looked as though he had just happened to catch a glimpse of someone passing by. The person was seen in a landscape or a room that revealed something about him; he looked absorbed in his work or his thoughts, not in the process of having his picture taken. Musicians realized right away that Dean's pictures were truer representations than the standard studio portraits and hired him to take their publicity shots. They were among his first customers. The others were the people of Cranberry Island. We had gone to that wild Maine island in the summer of 1965. Dean had set up a temporary darkroom in our cold summer house. We had spent days together hiking over the island, photographing and painting, exuberant at being away from the city for so long. Dean sold the pictures on the dock for two dollars apiece. It was a fine summer, a preview of things to come.

After the decision to quit music was made, we moved into a loft in downtown Manhattan where Dean could build a permanent darkroom. From then on, whenever we were in the city, Dean spent most of his waking hours in the darkroom. At first he built it to process black-and-white printing alone, but in 1969 he modified it to handle dye-transfer printing, and from then on he kept transforming it into a more perfect color lab. He built some of the equipment himself—the rocker tables, the light tables, the drying racks. He rebuilt some of the preexisting equipment and invented a few things. He was a perfectionist in his printing techniques, although again he took this dedication for granted. He claimed he hated having to spend so much time on the developing, that he did it only because he could achieve accuracy no other way. When young photographers asked him how to learn to print, he told them they should read the Ansel Adams books, follow all the procedures, and then establish their own simplified methods. Once he wrote to a friend: "The freedom that used to come from long struggle with learning hard techniques just doesn't happen anymore, because everyone goes for the freedom first. And it's great, when it works. It just doesn't work for very many people." Everything he did in photography was based on a rock-solid mastery of the craft, although typically he never talked about it. He felt that if someone called himself a photographer, he should know what he was doing. He felt he had to learn to walk in order to learn to run. He said, "I was trained in the Euclidean sense: this can be done, that can be done. I like geometry, hypotheses."

When he was asked to write a biographical statement for George Eastman House in 1968, he reluctantly produced the following:

> *Began photographing at age 10; continued sporadically until 1960. Most prints and negatives destroyed; most all work very bad. Married a painter in 1960, and although I was heavily involved in graduate work in musicology,*

I began to redevelop and renew my interest; "discovered" Weston and Cartier-Bresson around 1963 and began again, gradually dissolving my connections with musicology and college teaching of music. Became full-time free-lance photographer in June 1967. I suppose I want to do what anyone else wants to do: produce images that are beautiful, personal, and meaningful. I know a little about what I don't want to produce: pictures that depend on slick or accepted technique . . .

The closest I have come to studying is reading The Day Books of Edward Weston *and receiving advice and criticism from my wife, a painter, and Duane Michals, a photographer whose work I had liked for several years and whom I only recently met.*

No formal education (photographic). I have read (desultorily) various technical works, the most important being the Ansel Adams' The Negative *and* The Print. *This was enough, as far as I am concerned, for technique, and I can choose to use it or not, depending on the image I want. As for aesthetic education, I simply look at other people's photographs and paintings, and see a great many movies.*

Throughout his life, Dean used the 35mm camera almost exclusively. The rare exceptions were technical shots that required a 4″ × 5″ view camera or a 2¼″ × 2¼″ twin-lens reflex. For a time, he shot mainly in black-and-white and tried different ways of printing. He shot the funeral of Martin Luther King from the television screen and then printed it in extreme high contrast on Kodalith film. The results were stark and moving. Dean described them in these words: " . . . I have tried to show what I feel about the South (mostly outrage and a compassion for the people I grew up with)."

By 1969, he had arrived at a way of shooting and printing that was distinctly his own. He wanted to capture the most detail possible about a person or a place. He therefore used the smallest lens opening and the slowest shutter speed to achieve the greatest depth of field. He used wide-angle lenses much more than telephoto, again because they recorded greater detail. In fact, he spent a long time working with the fisheye lens, de-emphasizing the distortions and concentrating on its ability to encompass more information.

He printed the pictures small, just 4″ × 6″. He had technical and aesthetic reasons for that choice: "Some people have been put off by—or failed to really see the images because of—the small size. . . . I am very sensitive about the point where the image begins to break up and lose tone scale because of the discontinuity inherent in the grain of the film." He wanted crystal clarity as well as the intimacy of the small size. He printed full-frame and with the widest tonal range. He used a glossy paper but did not ferrotype it, so the detail was crisp but the surface had a soft sheen instead of a mechanical glare. His pictures were meant for quiet and careful contemplation.

From 1967 to 1969, he was still making portraits. Now, however, his subjects were more famous—Joan Sutherland, Edward Villella, Beverly Sills, Thomas Hart Benton. (He continued to take portraits throughout his career. After 1969, they were often in color and of people in more varied walks of life—President and Mrs. Lyndon Johnson, Robert Redford, Ron Carter, Ima Hogg.) He was shooting photo essays for *New York Magazine*—Jamaican cricket teams on Staten Island, authors living on welfare, the arrival of the Temple of Dendur at the Brooklyn docks. Over a period of several months, he made a portfolio of a couple named John and Mimi making love. They were photographed in the same direct and natural way that Dean photographed any other subject. Hence, they struck some people as being very shocking. He made a portfolio of the desolation of the Lower West Side of Manhattan. (In 1973, he made another black-and-white portfolio of a ruined section of the city, this time East New York.)

Dean did a series of photo essays on opera houses for *Opera News*. He expanded these assignments to include a great deal more than just the buildings. The one on opera in San Antonio included the whole town. The results of his exploration of the rambling grounds of the Music Academy of the West in California became his first published landscape portfolio. Finally, in November 1969, he went to Berlin to photograph the opera houses of both the eastern and western sectors. He was left with the following impression:

I had always believed Berlin to be a very busy, cosmopolitan place; instead I found a beautiful, rebuilt city with very few inhabitants. Very lonely–like a giant sleeping. I was amazed at the landscape in Berlin–so many parks, even whole forests, lakes, rivers. But if West Berlin was lonely, East Berlin was like a desert. . . . Berlin is so much parkland. All carefully groomed and glittering in the late fall light that seems to hang around four o'clock all day when there is no smog. And there is, even in the busy areas, a feeling of loneliness, emptiness. The city lost over a million people during the war, and perhaps the ones left spend all their time indoors working.

In the Berlin pictures, Dean achieved that perfect coincidence of craft with content. There was a richness of detail and black-and-white tonal range and a meticulous attention to composition. There was a sense of the tragedy of postwar Germany. The photographs were haunting.

Dean was now ready to fully tackle color photography. Color is much more difficult to use well than black-and-white. When it is mishandled, it can easily lead to chaotic results. Dean was so keenly aware of this that he almost never shot color and black-and-white film of the same subject for fear of desensitizing his eye for one or the other.

Dean used Kodachrome II film almost exclusively because it gave the richest color and was the most reliable. However, it was also very slow (ASA 25), so he had to use a heavy tripod almost all the time, even on wilderness treks, in order to achieve the great depth of field he preferred. The color balance of the film was affected at certain times of day when he had to use long exposures. The film itself was fragile and required intricate precautions to protect it from heat and dampness. And finally, there was the problem of making prints.

Kodachrome II (subsequently replaced by Kodachrome 25) was color positive film, which when developed produced 35mm slides. Three types of prints could be made from the slides—R, C, and dye-transfer. The R- and C-type prints, although much easier and cheaper to produce, simply did not look like the slides from which they were made. Only dye-transfer prints retained the accuracy and brilliance of the original color. Dye transfer, the most difficult of all the printing methods, requires meticulous, painstaking labor. Dean decided that he had to learn to do it.

He had started shooting extensively in color shortly before the trip to Berlin. We had gone to California in the spring of 1969. It was Dean's first trip to the West, although I had been there many times. On the way back, I introduced him briefly to the northwestern part of Arizona and the southern part of Utah. He resolved to go back as soon as possible. His decision to shoot in color was inextricably linked to his decision to concentrate on landscape. The open space and the brilliance of the color in the West made him feel as though he had, until then, been looking at the world from inside a small box with dark windows. He began to dislike the city: " . . . I live in New York and daily suffer the masses of people everywhere—like swimming in some massive, dirty stream. Every day in the summer when you come home, you jump into the shower because you have spent the day in that mass of dirt, sweat, indifference, and insults."

We returned to the West in the summer of 1969. Dean had an assignment to shoot the coastline of California from Oregon to Mexico. We then went to the western part of the Navajo Reservation in Arizona in order to work in the high desert. Besides painting and camera gear, our equipment included United States Geological Survey maps, a compass, other necessities for desert survival, and an ice chest for the film. We got up before dawn in order to be ready for the first light. We worked until the heat drove us out, about 11:00 A.M. Then we took shelter, ate, and slept. We came out again around 4:00 P.M. and stayed out until after sunset. We even spent some nights working in the dark. Dean set up the cameras on tripods and made twenty-minute exposures of spots he had preselected during the day.

We became acutely sensitive to light. When you are making a picture of a landscape without people or animals in it, there is no anecdote to make it interesting. The earth itself is the subject and the changes of light provide the fascination. The more we worked with landscape, the more interested we became in geology. To Dean, who had always loved codes, geology was another code: If you can decipher the walls of a canyon, you can understand its history.

Dean considered the picture complete when he clicked the shutter. When he made the final print, his aim was to reproduce the slide as carefully as possible. He didn't manipulate the picture or the scene. Even in his portrait work, he used available light and did not pose his subjects. Any scene in nature changes according to the interconnected factors of weather, season, and light. Pictures taken of the scene vary according to the lens, film, and camera used and to where the photographer stands. Dean would endure any hardship to be in the right place at the right time. He explained his approach this way: "I got used to trying to get the essential character of a person onto film; I try to do the same with landscape."

He once sat motionless for days beside a pond in Alaska, being eaten by mosquitos that were immune to repellent, in order to get the right shot of Blackwater Pond. While he was there, he became very sensitive to everything going on around him. He saw a wolf daily picking off baby ducks. He knew that bears came and went. He also knew that his presence during those few days had altered the life there. Many of his pictures were taken at spots selected after he had hiked off the trail over extremely difficult terrain for many hours. He would lie on the ground or stand in a river up to his waist or balance on a ledge to be in the right position. The passion to get the unique shot and the ability to know what was unique made him an artist rather than just a competent craftsman.

Once an editor and a writer accompanied him on a free-lance assignment to illustrate a book—a situation very unusual and very uncomfortable for Dean. Both carried cameras to take tourist shots, so they said. They plagued him by asking him for meter readings. As soon as he left a spot, they stood where he had stood and took their own pictures. When they returned to New York, they used their pictures instead of Dean's throughout the book. They didn't have his eye for framing or his concern for clarity, but since they had been standing where he had stood, using his meter readings and covering the same general area, their pictures sufficed for the purpose. It was moral, if not legal, plagiarism. Anyone can click a shutter to record a scene on film, but where and when and how a photographer chooses to do it is at the heart of his originality.

Some months after our trip to Arizona, Dean and I were to have a show at the Witkin Gallery in New York, displaying the work we had done in the desert. Dean read all the literature he could find on dye-transfer printing in order to learn how to do it. He talked to Bob Speck, the inventor of the method. He spent arduous months modifying his darkroom and gathering materials. Finally, he printed the pictures for the show. It was an extraordinary achievement. Dean said of it:

> *I have gained a new insight, as well as respect, for the problems of printers since learning dye-transfer. (I learned it from scratch and printed the pictures in five weeks–the most hellish five weeks I have ever spent.) What I love most, though, is that if your separation negs are anywhere near right, the first proof of a dye comes so much closer to the chrome than most R or C prints can ever do. And from then on, it's usually better and better. Kind of satisfying after all that one has to go through to set up for dyes. As I may have mentioned earlier, it's not doing the dyes that is so hard, it's trying to find all the materials, setting up, and then having incredible patience.*

The prints for the Witkin show were jewel-like, precise, brilliant. The color had a richness and subtlety not often seen in color photographs, because these qualities are often sacrificed for a jarring garishness that is easier to reproduce in magazines and hence easier to sell. At this point, Dean had arrived at a way of working in color that was distinctly his own. He was being included in important photographic exhibitions. He was getting enough portrait and still-life assignments to feel less worried about finances. He wrote to a friend: "... as long as I can live on some kind of non-obnoxious commercial work and get time to shoot for myself, that's all I care about. Being a known 'art-photographer,' social lion, or raconteur doesn't appeal to me." We both wanted to do more work in the wilderness.

Dean's way of photographing changed as his skill at shooting in a wide range of wilderness conditions increased. One of the keys to his exuberance was that he set himself difficult challenges and then gathered all his forces to meet them. In Arizona in 1969, he was learning how to use color film and how to work in intense heat, wind, and sand. The resulting pictures had a direct simplicity. In 1970, he learned how to cope with radical weather changes while shooting. In late summer, he started to photograph gardens in Philadelphia for Time-Life Books and ended up in Denver in November, having worked through Dallas, San Antonio, Tucson, Los Angeles, Seattle, and several other cities along the way. It was snowing in Denver and he was still wearing the summer clothes he'd started out with. He bought himself a down jacket, finished up the job, and then met me in Albuquerque. We took off in a rented car for Utah and the Burr Trail. Dean was learning how to shoot nature the way a reporter shoots news events—moving quickly to be in the right place at the right time and shooting under any conditions, oblivious to everything except getting the right shot. This was a change from the way he had shot in Arizona, where he had been taking pictures that had a static purity: The sand dunes looked as though they had been that way for centuries and would remain so.

Now he worked towards getting on film those moments which show the basic character of a place, but which also show that everything is always changing. A study of geology had impressed on him how transitory earth forms are. A greater understanding of life had convinced him that the only permanent thing is death. As a result, the city became more oppressive to him than ever. He complained that it never changed, that he could barely tell one season from another, that it was a totally synthetic environment that sapped all vitality.

In the spring of 1971, we backpacked through the Indian ruins of the Southwest and down into the Grand Canyon. We were going farther into remote areas for longer periods of time. The freedom from the concern about whether we could get back to the road by night allowed us to see things most people miss: the cliffs of the back country at Bandelier, New Mexico, blazing white under the full moon; on later trips, the mountains and desert of the Papago Reservation suddenly turning a brilliant yellow moments before a storm; ice gardens translucent in the night sun at Glacier Bay, Alaska.

We went to Alaska that summer. We felt that we had never seen wilderness until then. We walked on land that in all likelihood no human being had ever walked on before. We saw birds and animals in such profusion and of such vigor that we began to think of wild areas that we had seen in the lower forty-eight as being tragically impoverished. It was exhilarating to see such immense beauty. Dean worked day and night, getting almost no sleep, in order not to miss the light. He wanted to get Alaska itself on film, not just pretty pictures. Before he had left on the assignment, he had written: "My main effort in photographing landscape is to achieve a sense of place." And so we hiked, boated, and flew over Glacier Bay, Mount McKinley, the Brooks Range, the North Slope, and Katmai. We returned with the liberating thought that the triumphs and tragedies of people are simply not that important in relation to the vastness of the universe.

For a time after Alaska we retrenched. Dean was working in the darkroom on the dye transfers. He was trying to get enough free-lance assignments so that we could move out of New York. He was studying Eskimo because he wanted to go back to Alaska. Then, in the spring of 1972, we went to Italy and Japan. We were in Italy for only ten days and spent the time looking at paintings, not photographing or painting. In Japan, we went to the fish market in Tokyo, the temples in Kyoto, and the wilderness areas in Hokkaido. Dean photographed extensively. He felt comfortable with the language and with the visual delights of the gardens, the food, the markets, and the baths. Roaming Hokkaido in a rented car was an adventure during which we finally saw the kinds of landscape that appeared in the paintings we had both studied for years.

Back to New York and then, in August, back to Arizona, this time to the Sonoran Desert on assignment for Time-Life Books. We were working under adverse conditions. Dean wrote:

> *. . . They sent me out to southern Arizona in midsummer when the temperature was 115 degrees in the shade, and I had to backpack into canyons and up mountains carrying as much as sixty-five pounds (because of the need to carry all the water I would need); while there I enjoyed sudden thunderstorms, blinding sandstorms, and got bitten by the so-called "deadly" scorpion. Although most of the editors down there have little idea just what sort of irritation and hardship this sort of thing entails, it nevertheless demonstrates that I can produce when the going gets rough.*

He came back with pictures that showed the fresh morning stillness after a violent night's sandstorm and the strange light over vast spaces before a thunderstorm.

A few months later, Dean returned alone to

the Canyon de Chelly. He had learned to speak some Navajo by then and was able to wander freely around the rim and into the canyon. He slept out by Spider Rock and captured on film the first and last rays of sun lighting the rock walls. He pointed his camera at the sky.

That fall, back in New York, we discovered that an hour away from the city there are hundreds of miles of trails through back country at Harriman State Park and Bear Mountain. Every weekend, no matter what the weather, we went there to hike. The bones of the land are not revealed openly there as they are in the West. It is a very subtle landscape. Objects do not stand out clearly. There are not many clear views of vast space and those which do exist are hazy. The sky is not vivid. Most of the interest lies in trees, grasses, and lakes. There is an overall delicacy in the profusion of branches, leaves, shadows, and dappled light. Dean shot there with a tender appreciation of the land that gave us a retreat, and these pictures are perhaps his most personal.

Spring of 1973 took us first to Texas. Dean had been there before to shoot the wild flowers on the LBJ Ranch and the restored stone houses of the hill country. Now he was to document a large section of the LBJ Ranch that had been sold for development and for parkland. There were rocky cliffs down to the Pedernales River, rolling ranch land with clusters of live oaks, and acres of brilliant wild flowers. There were cattle, of course, but also gazelles, ibex, big-horned sheep, and many other foreign hoofed animals that would flash through the trees and leave us to wonder what had passed.

We had one last trip to Arizona—one week away from assignments and the city. We spent part of it alone in a secret canyon. The afternoon we walked into it, Dean declared it paradise. There were cottonwoods, birds, a cold stream, and many animals. The sounds were those of wind, water, and birds. The light, Dean said, was as he had remembered afternoon light during his childhood. He shot many rolls of film, but ironically they were all destroyed by water damage. The film, as usual, had been placed in a container in an ice chest to protect it from the intense heat. For the first time, the container had leaked. When Dean found out about it, he said, "Well, maybe that was right. Maybe it was too perfect to photograph."

A few weeks later, we were sent to New Hampshire on another wilderness assignment for Time-Life Books. The White Mountains are an immense granite formation of harsh beauty. Because of their structure and the violent weather conditions, they have claimed many lives. It began raining when we arrived, and for a week we backpacked up and down Mount Washington in driving, freezing rain. All of our equipment became damaged in some way. We became exhausted from the freezing nights out in the rain and the agonizing hikes up steep trails that had turned into waterfalls. The wind was a force we had to battle continuously. One night, we managed to hike out just before a heavy flood came that closed the mountain for days. In nearby areas, Dean shot the torrential streams and waterfalls. The rain did not stop and a national emergency was declared. Dean wrote the following note to the editors of Time-Life Books:

> *It's incredible up here. People are trapped on the mountain between streams so swollen with torrential rains that they cannot get down. Rescue teams are trying to bring them out with ropes; some of the huts are also isolated with no food and with scores of campers equally unprepared. We were very lucky to have chosen to escape when we did, or we might not have made it. . . . I just hope nobody dies up there today.*

Dean went on with the assignment. A geologist sent by Time-Life Books to advise him on what to shoot had pointed out a newly formed waterfall on Table Mountain. On the afternoon of July 5, Dean left me at the trail head. I thought that he was going to hike in and out quickly, getting a shot from the bottom of the mountain looking up at the waterfall. Evidently he decided that he could not get the picture he needed without climbing up the sheer, slick rock face. Around five o'clock the sky cleared for the first time. I knew that he would want to spend more time shooting. There was a sunset. At seven he fell.

The district ranger in charge of the rescue operation wrote the following: "Even though your husband was in extreme pain, at no time did he complain. When we had carried him nearly out, he was apologetic for the inconvenience he thought he was causing us. I have never known an individual so brave and strong under such severe circumstances. His behavior [revealed] everything in which to be proud."

DEAN BROWN

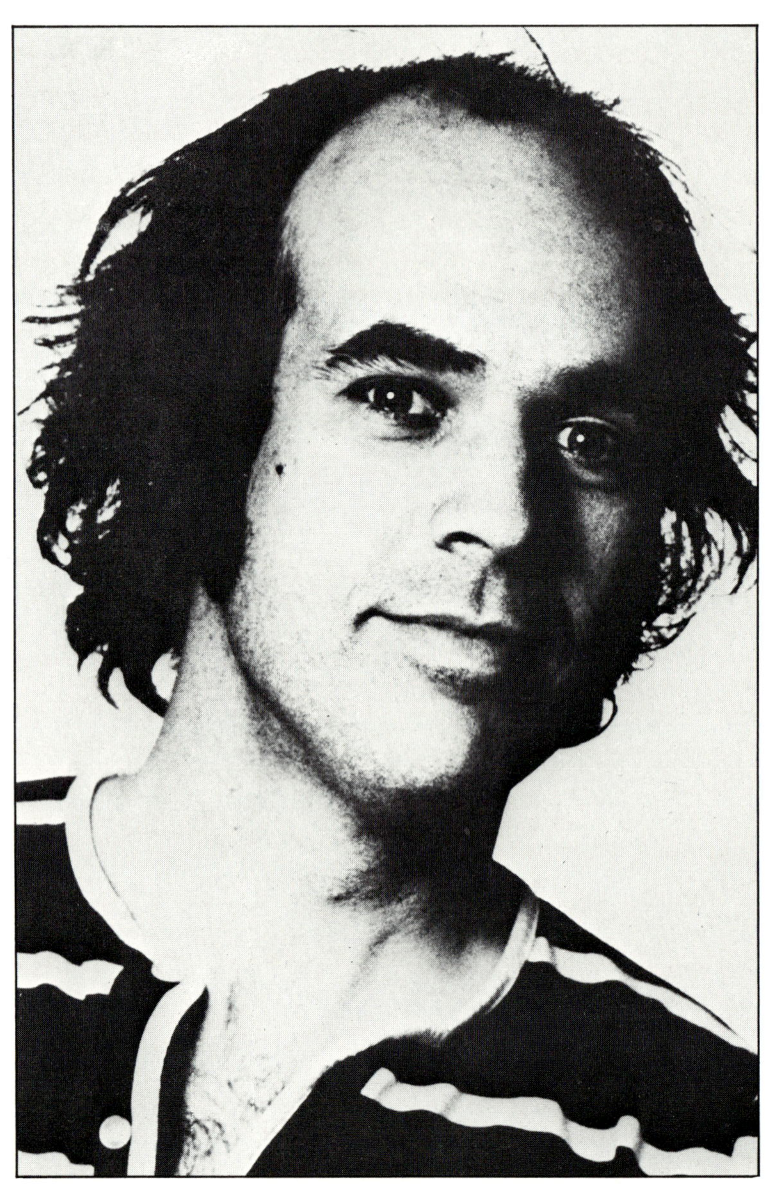

Born July 10, 1936 Newport News, Virginia
Died July 8, 1973 Portland, Maine

PERMANENT COLLECTIONS
Virginia Museum of Fine Arts, Richmond, Virginia
George Eastman House, Rochester, New York
University of Kansas Art Museum, Lawrence, Kansas
Victoria and Albert Museum, London, England
Canadian National Archives, Ottowa, Canada
C. J. Bucher, Lucerne, Switzerland

SOLO EXHIBITIONS
Akron Art Institute, Akron, Ohio
Virginia Museum of Fine Arts, Richmond, Virginia
Amon Carter Museum of Western Art, Fort Worth, Texas
Witte Memorial Museum, San Antonio, Texas
Krannert Art Museum, University of Illinois, Urbana, Illinois
Indianapolis Museum of Art, Indianapolis, Indiana

GROUP EXHIBITIONS
Whitney Museum, New York, New York ("Photography in America")
Virginia Museum of Fine Arts, Richmond, Virginia ("Virginia Photographers Exhibition—Certificate of Distinction")
George Eastman House, Rochester, New York ("Vision and Expression")
Yale University Art Gallery, New Haven, Connecticut ("Color Photography—Inventors and Innovators")
Witkin Gallery, New York, New York ("Dean Brown and Carol Brown")
Victoria and Albert Museum, London, England ("The Land")
National Gallery of Modern Art, Edinburgh, Scotland ("The Land")
Ulster Museum, Belfast, Ireland ("The Land")
National Museum of Wales, Cardiff, Wales ("The Land")

PUBLICATIONS IN WHICH DEAN BROWN'S WORK APPEARS
Photography in America by Robert Doty, Random House
Wild Places, Harper & Row
New England Wilds, Time-Life Books
Cactus Country, Time-Life Books
Wild Alaska, Time-Life Books
Landscape Gardening, Time-Life Books
The Print, Time-Life Books
Photographing Nature, Time-Life Books
The Art of Photography, Time-Life Books
Photography Annual 1974, Time-Life Books
Arts in Virginia, Spring 1974, Virginia Museum of Fine Arts
Camera, January 1973, November 1971, October 1971, July 1969
Art In America, No. One, 1971
Opera News, 1968–1973
House and Garden, 1971–1973
New York Magazine, 1968–1973

California

1
Near Solana Beach, California.
Cliffs down to the ocean.
August 1969

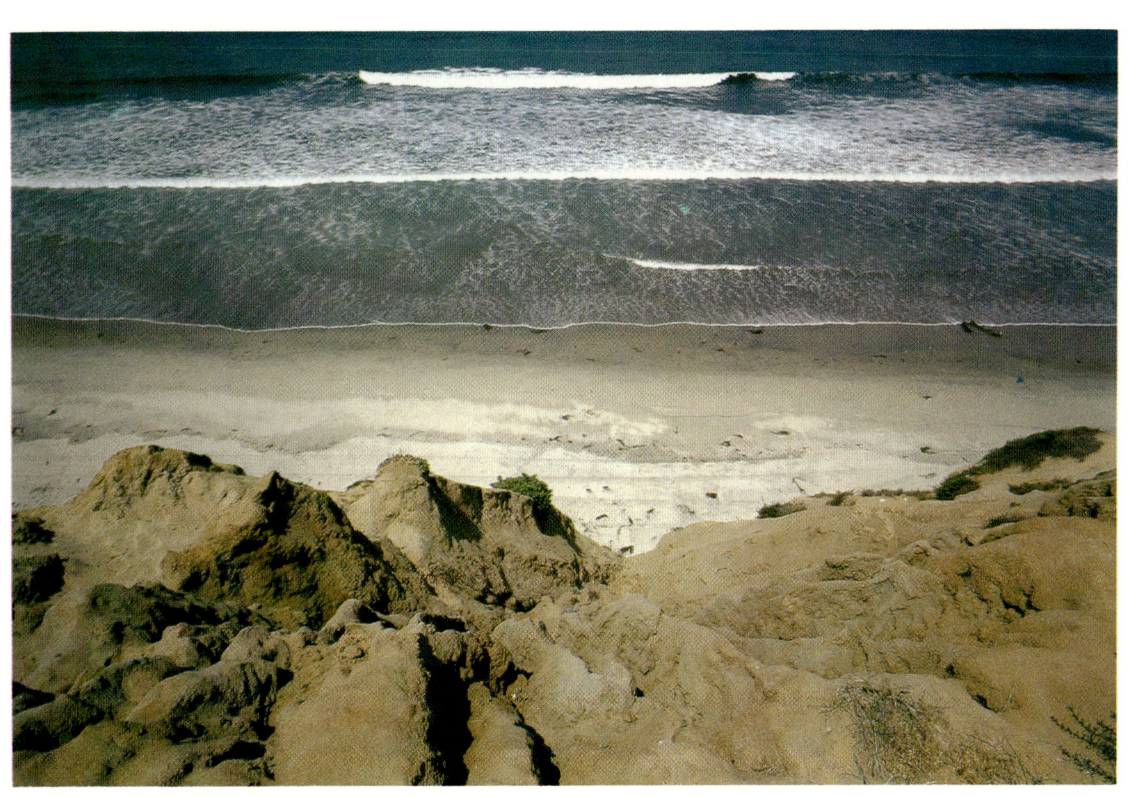

2

Near San Juan Capistrano, California.

Hillside.

August 1969

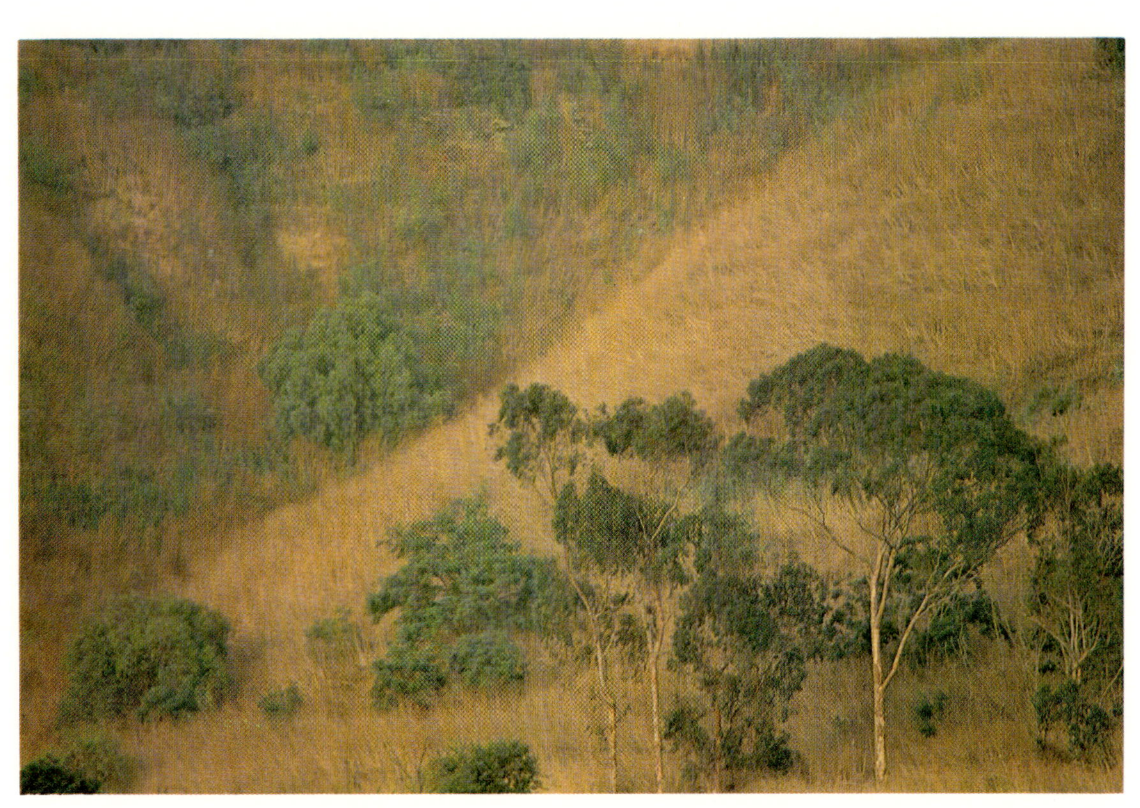

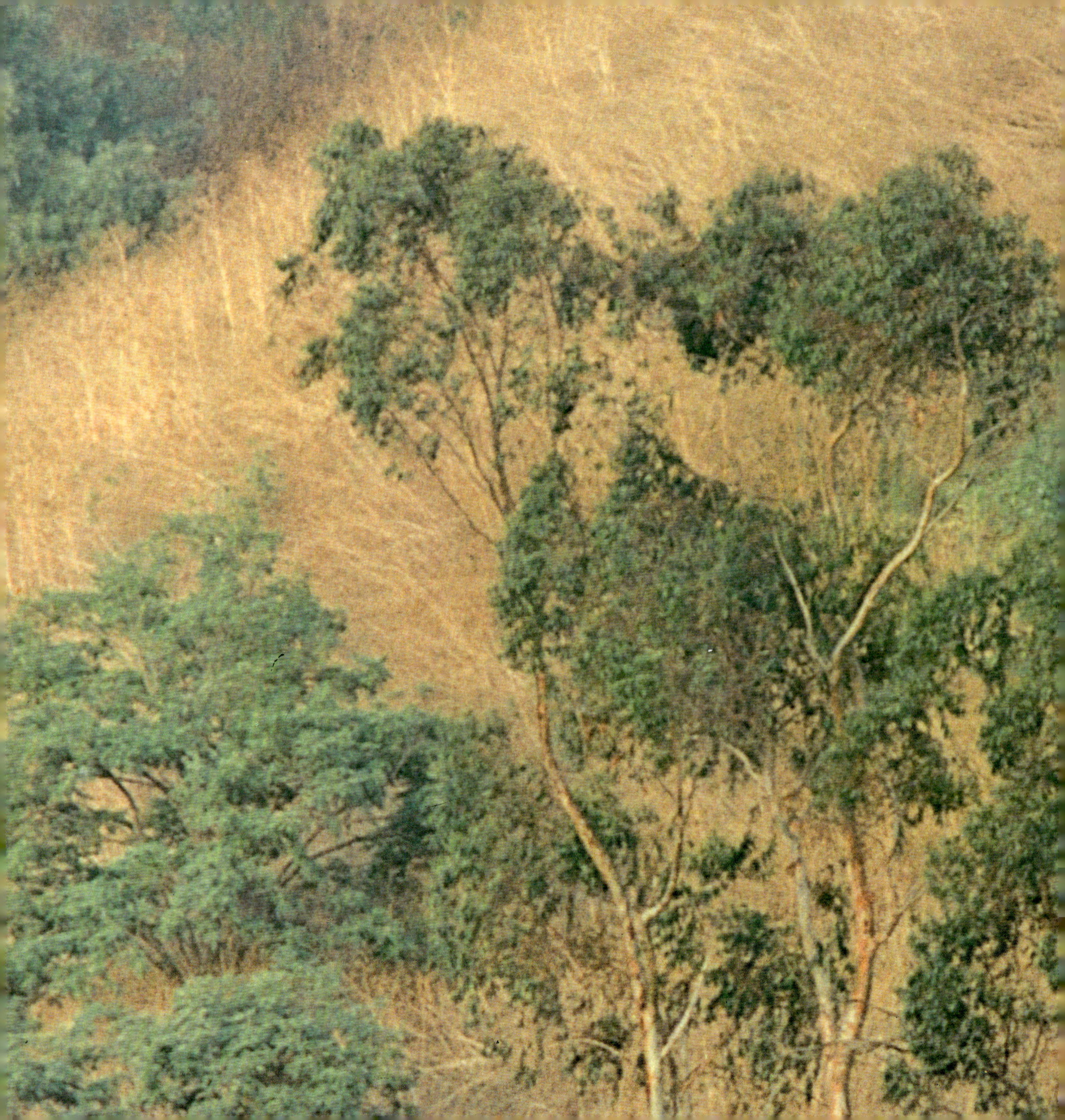

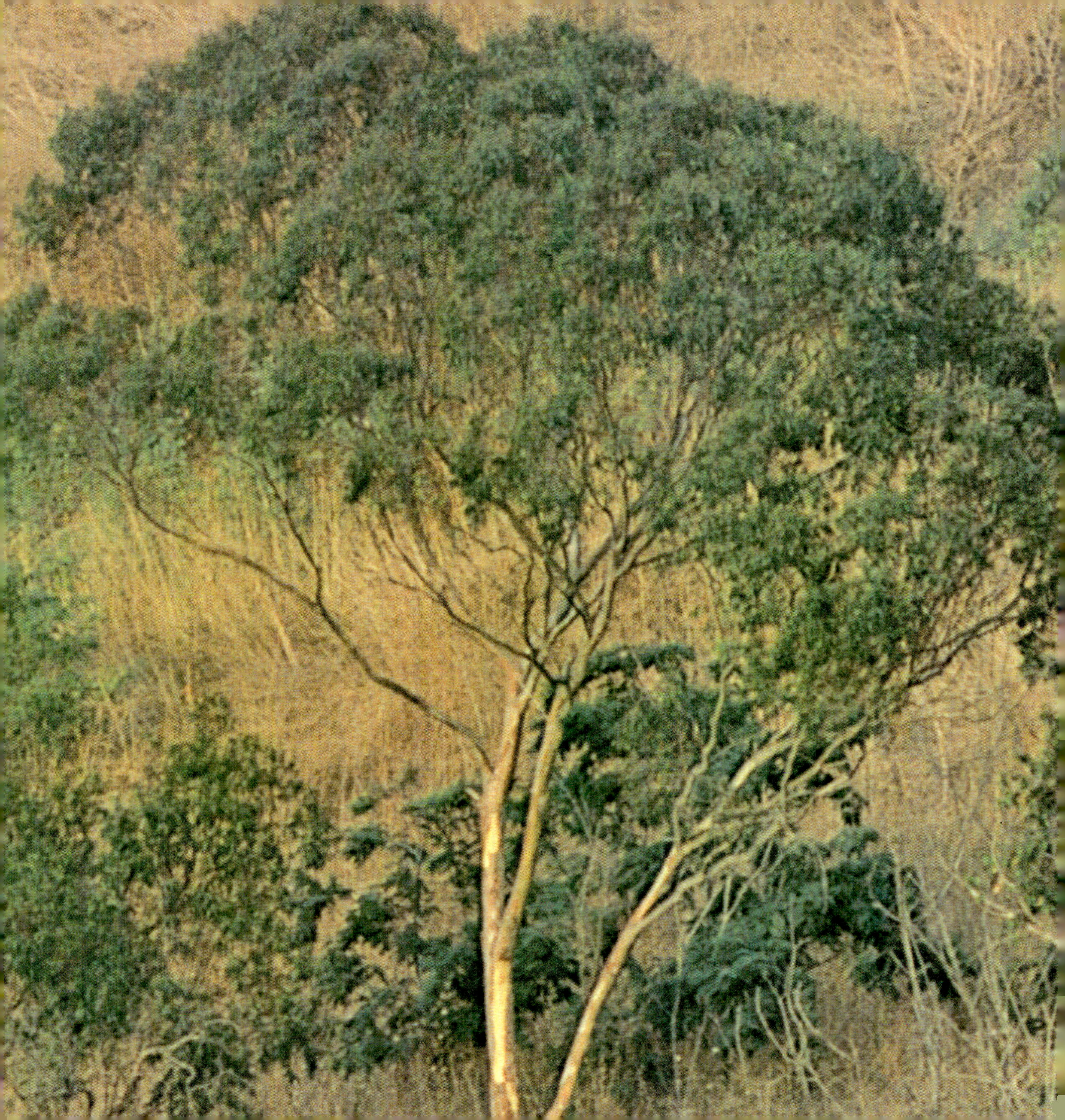

3

Between Crescent City and Klamath, California.

Fog.

August 1969

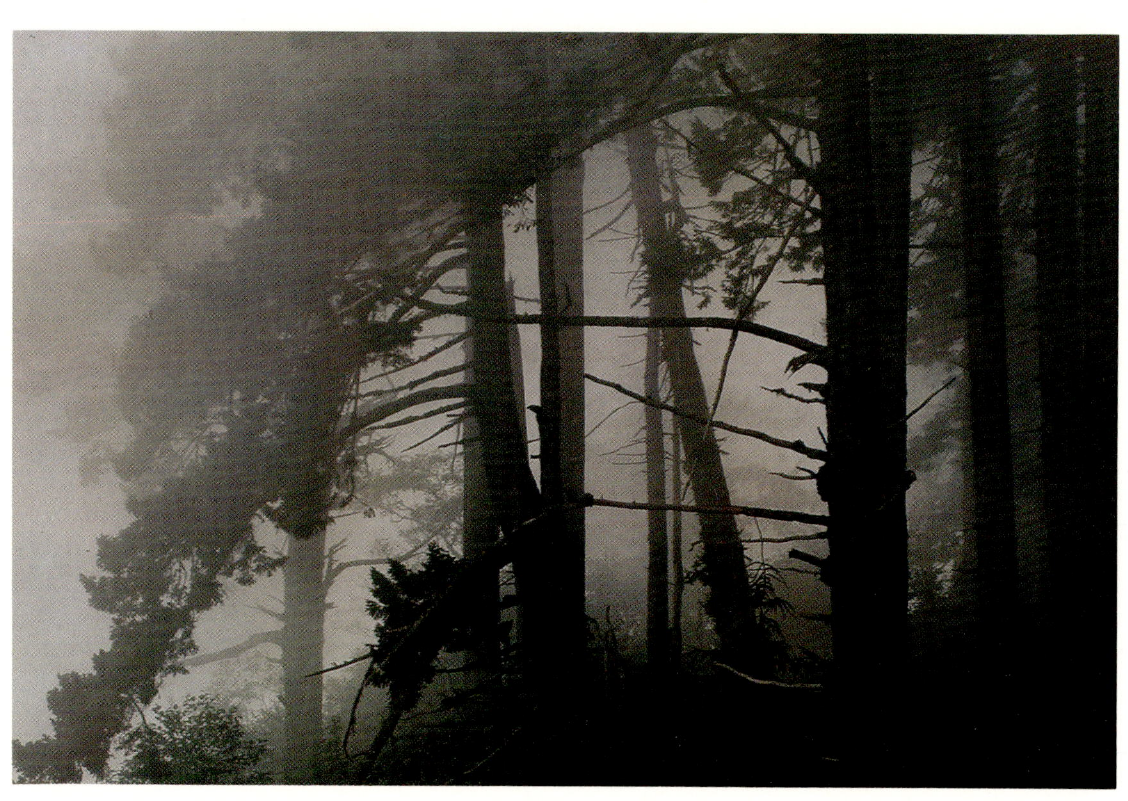

4

Near Crescent City, California.

Cows.

August 1969

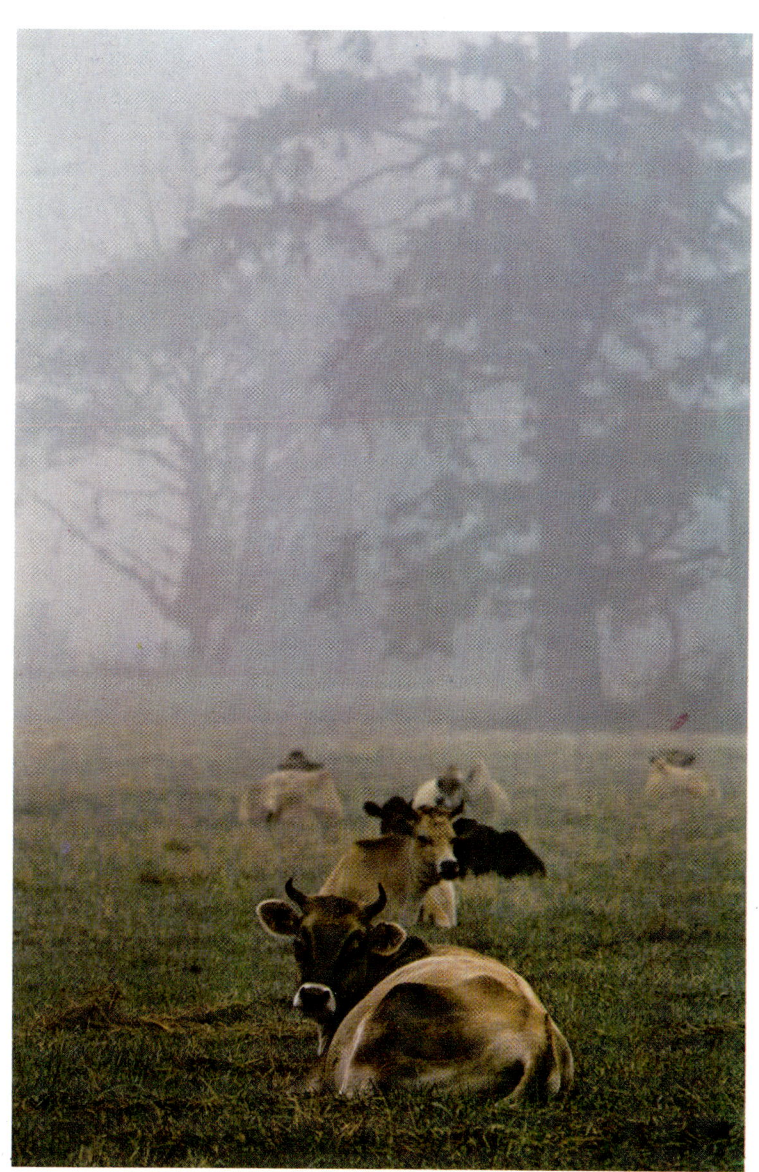

5

Pelican Beach, California.

Redwood stump in the Pacific Ocean.

August 1969

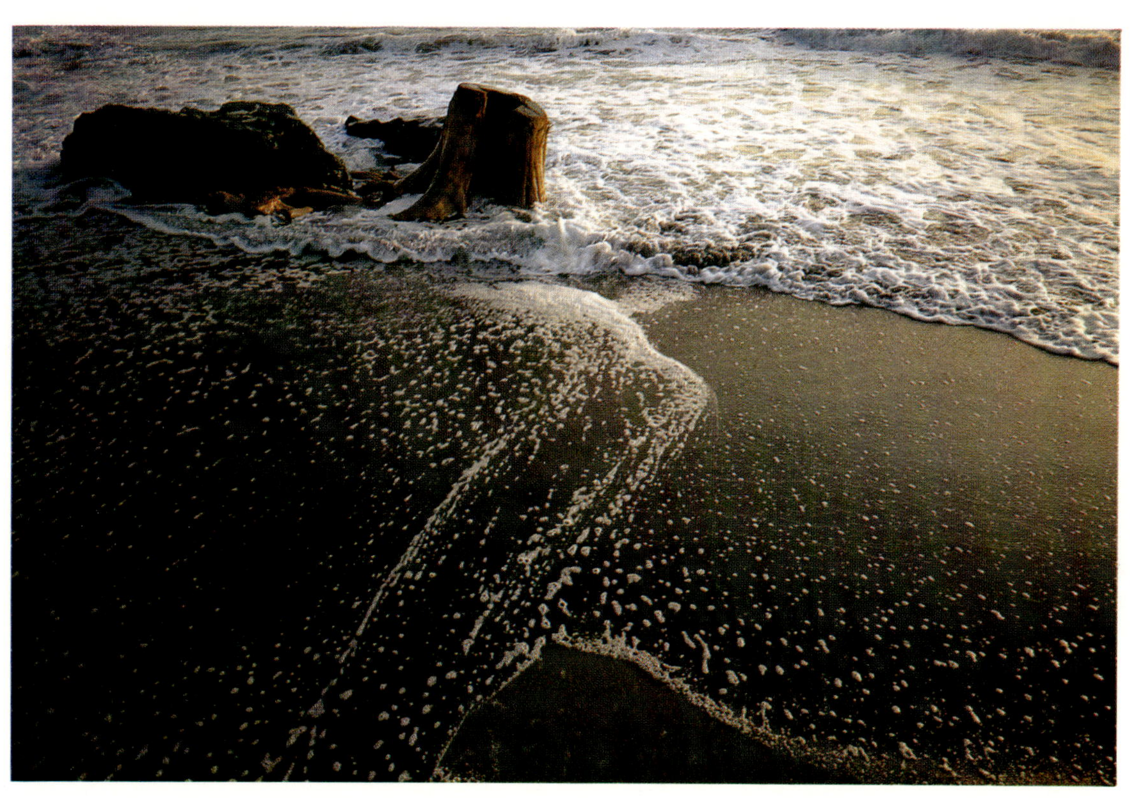

6

Death Valley, California.

Wind and sand.

February 1972

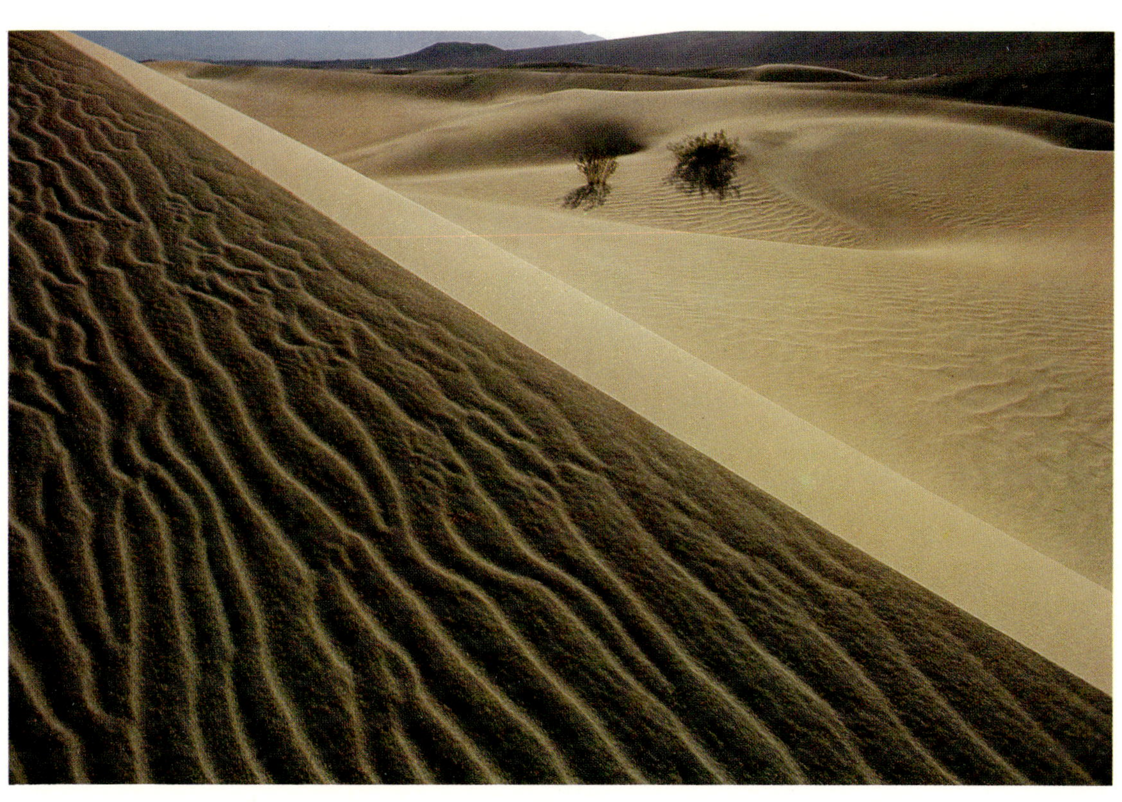

7

Death Valley, California.

Moon.

February 1972

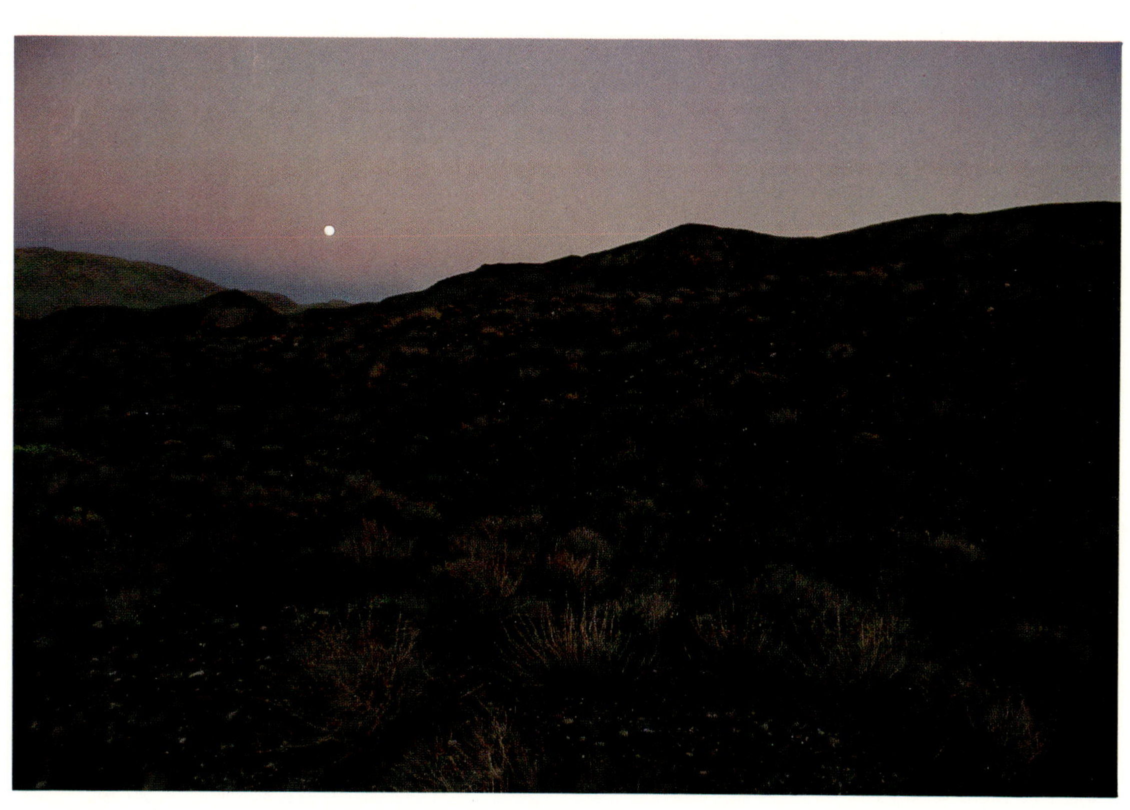

The Southwest

8
Navajo Reservation, Arizona.
Shadow Mountain.
August 1969

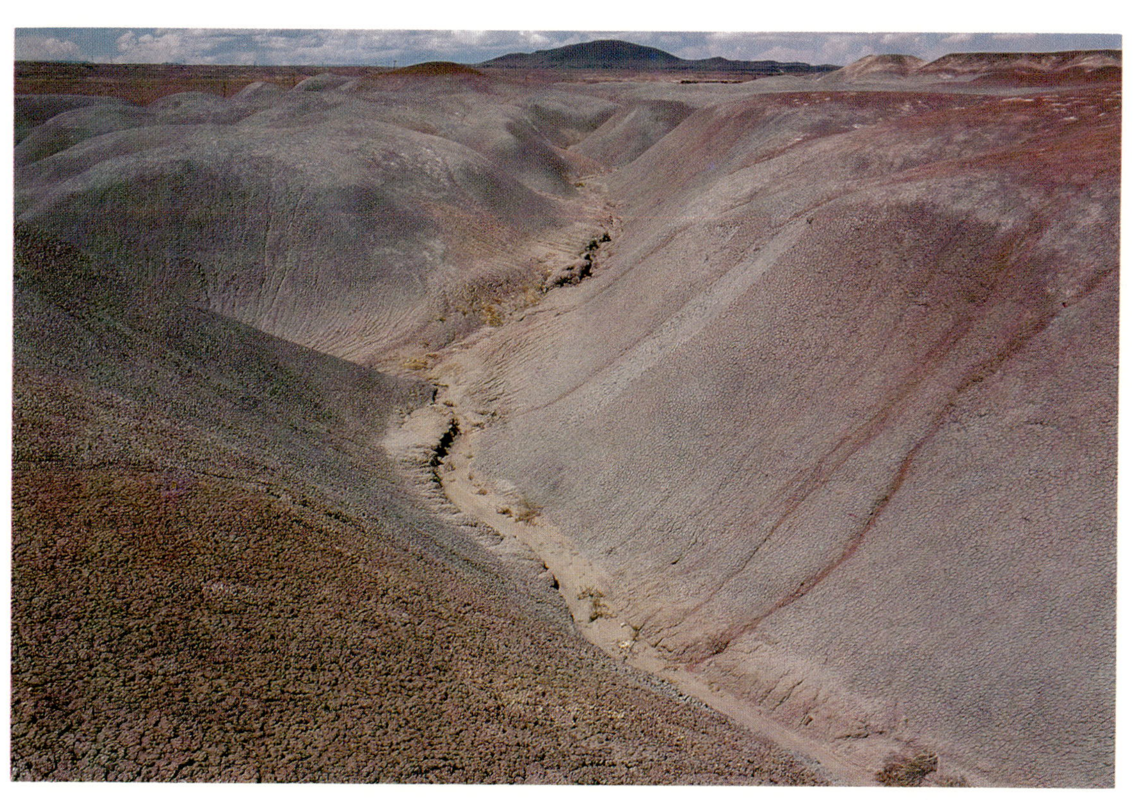

9

Navajo Reservation, Arizona.

Red hill.

August 1969

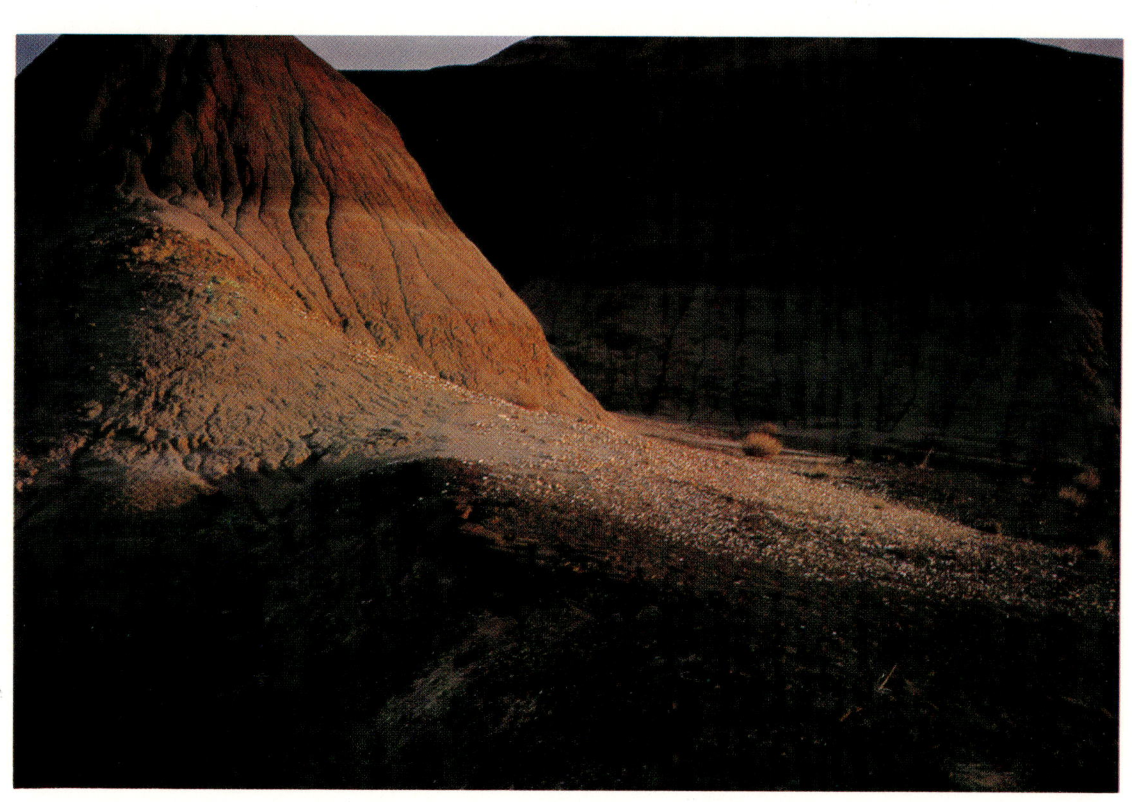

10
Navajo Reservation, Arizona.
Red striped hills.
August 1969

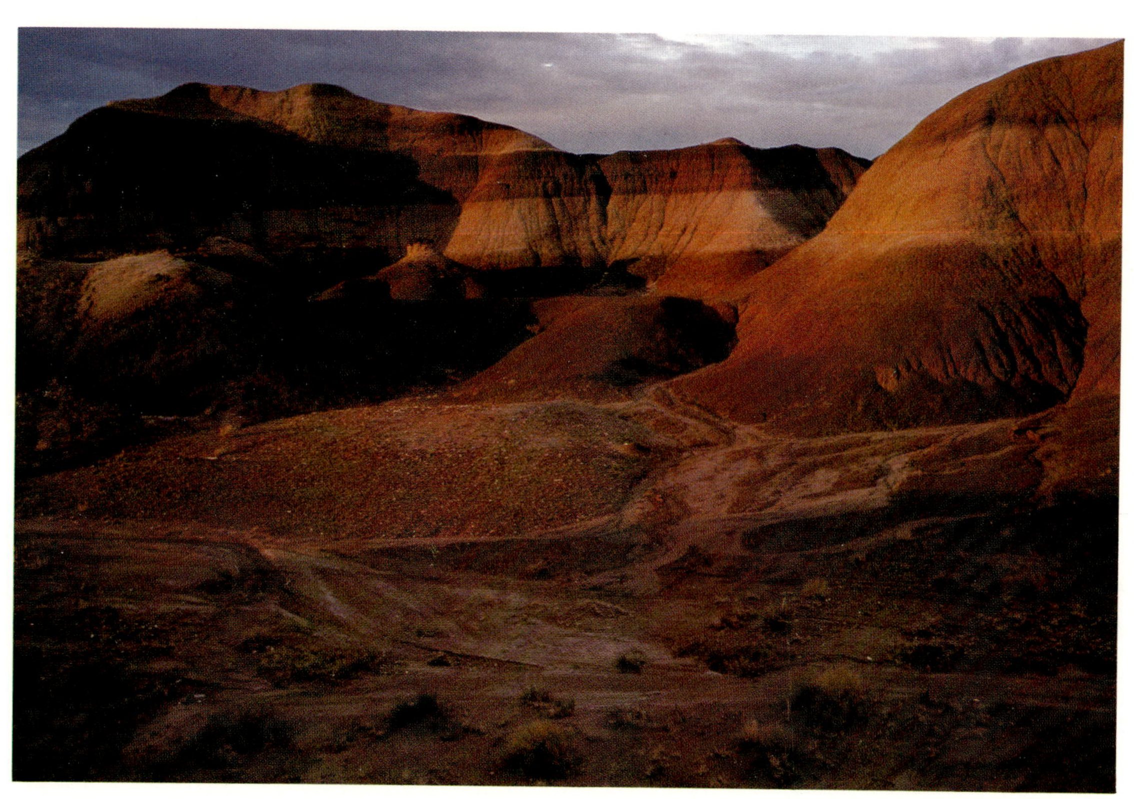

11

Navajo Reservation, Arizona.
Canyon de Chelly. South Rim.
November 1970

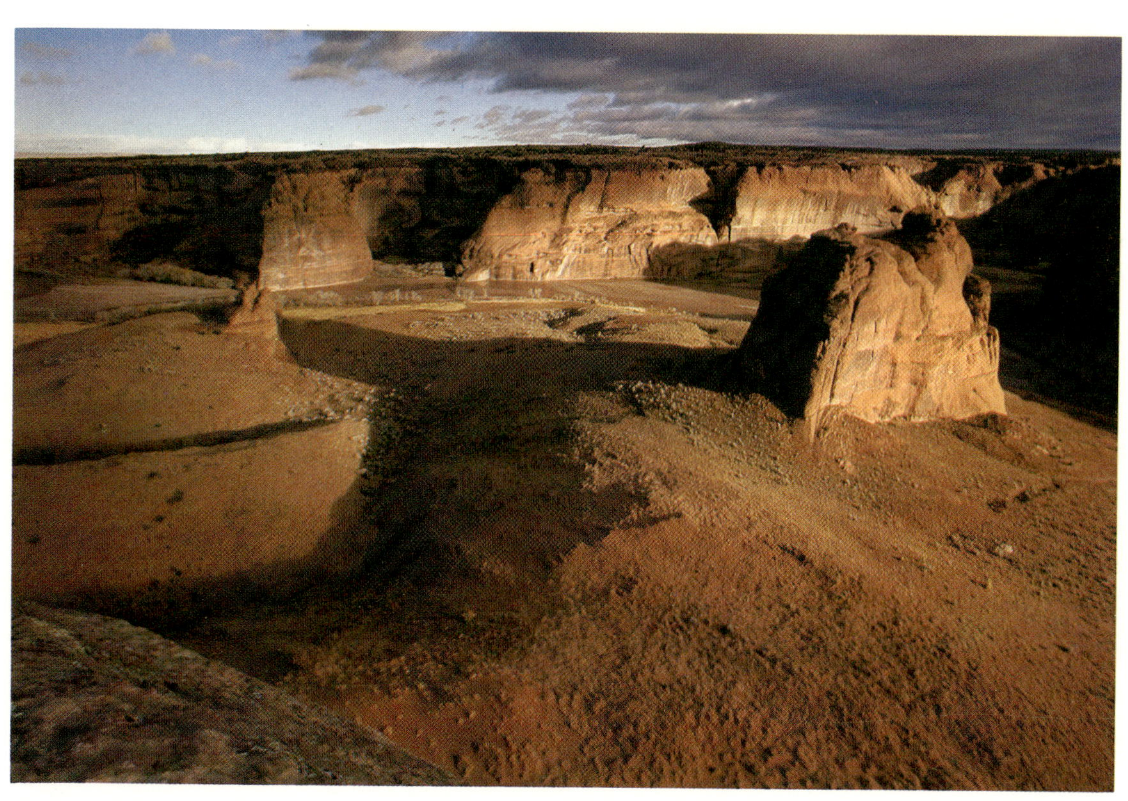

12
Navajo Reservation, Arizona.
Rio de Chelly.
November 1970

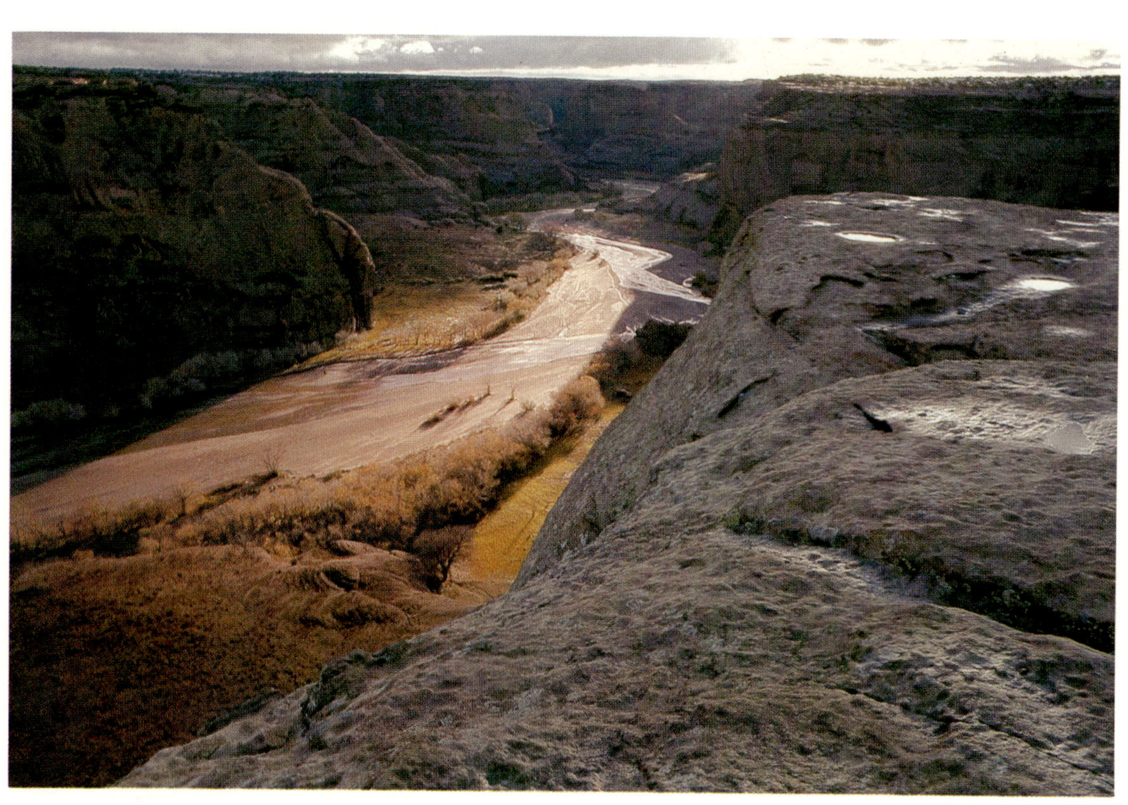

13

Navajo Reservation, Arizona.
Canyon de Chelly. Spider Rock.
October 1972

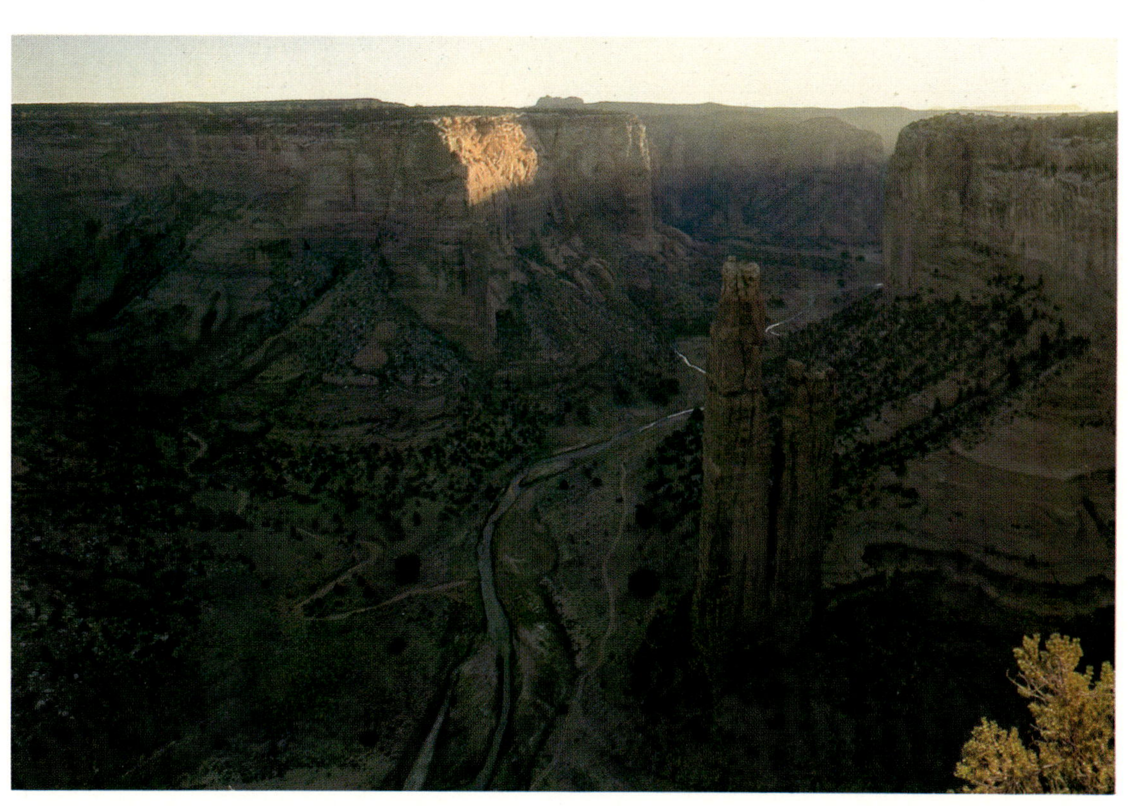

14
Navajo Reservation, Arizona.
Canyon wall and tree.
November 1970

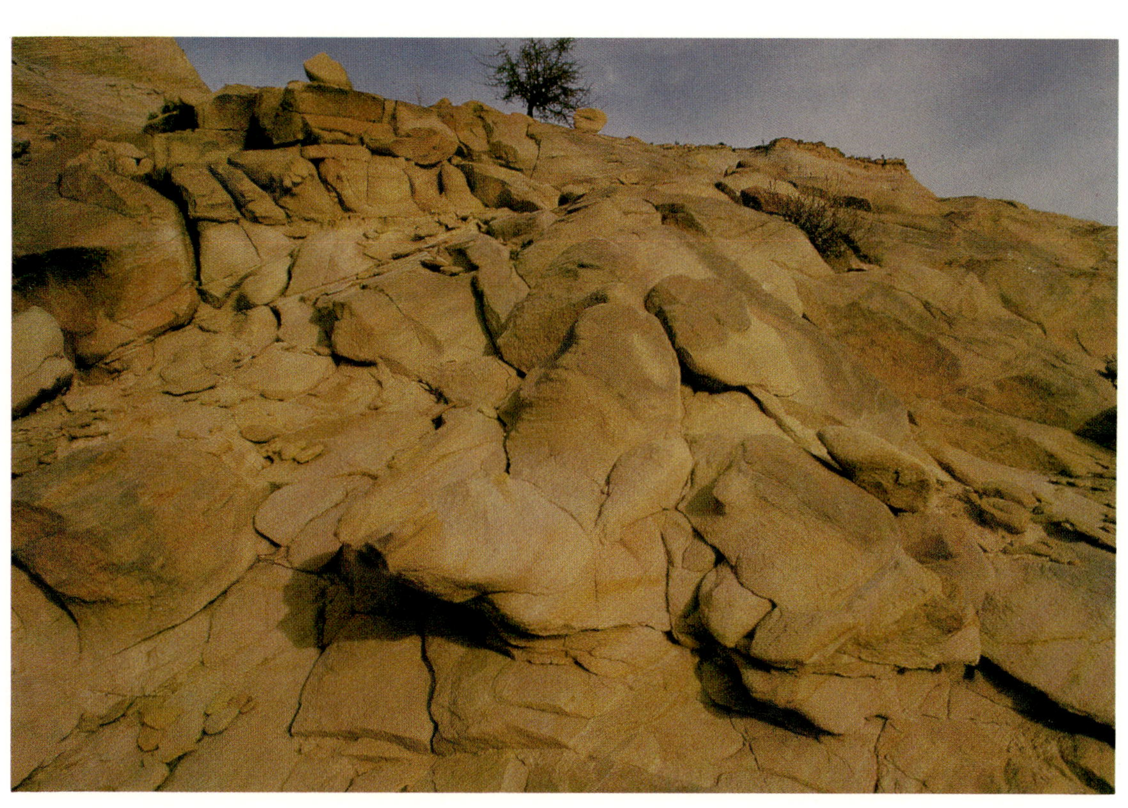

15

Navajo Reservation, Arizona.

Giddy sky.

October 1972

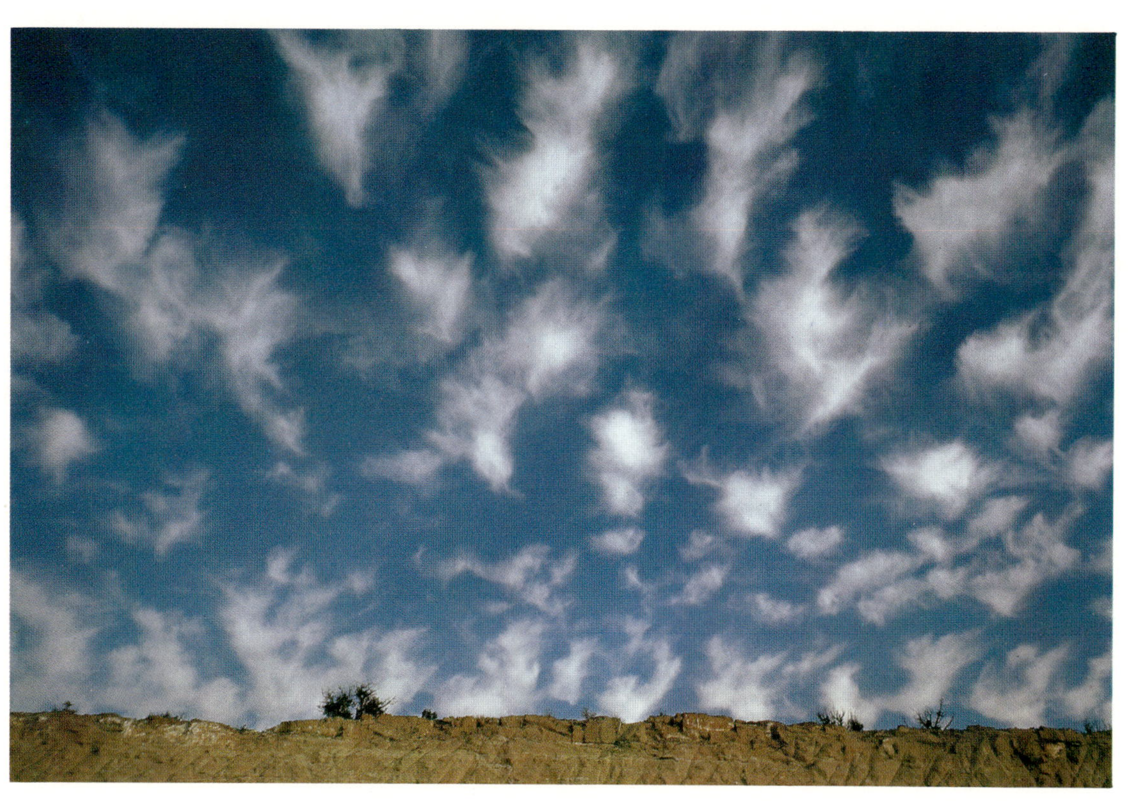

16

Lavalands, New Mexico.

October 1972

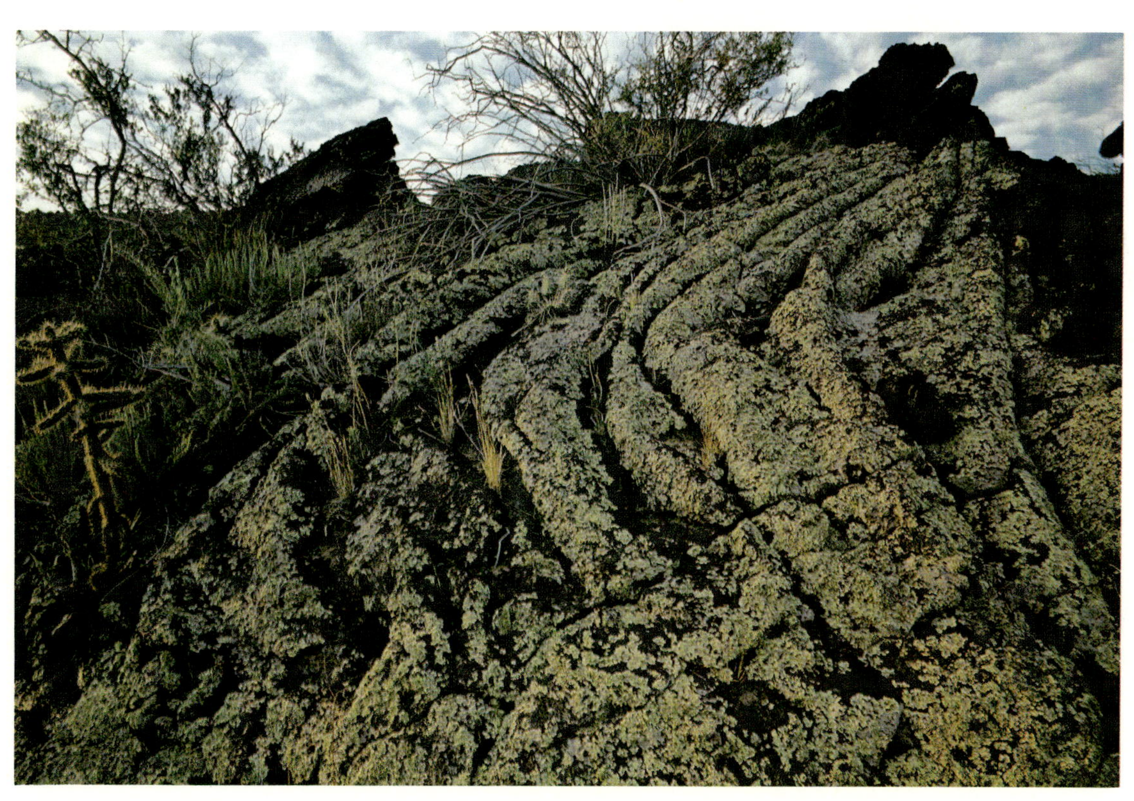

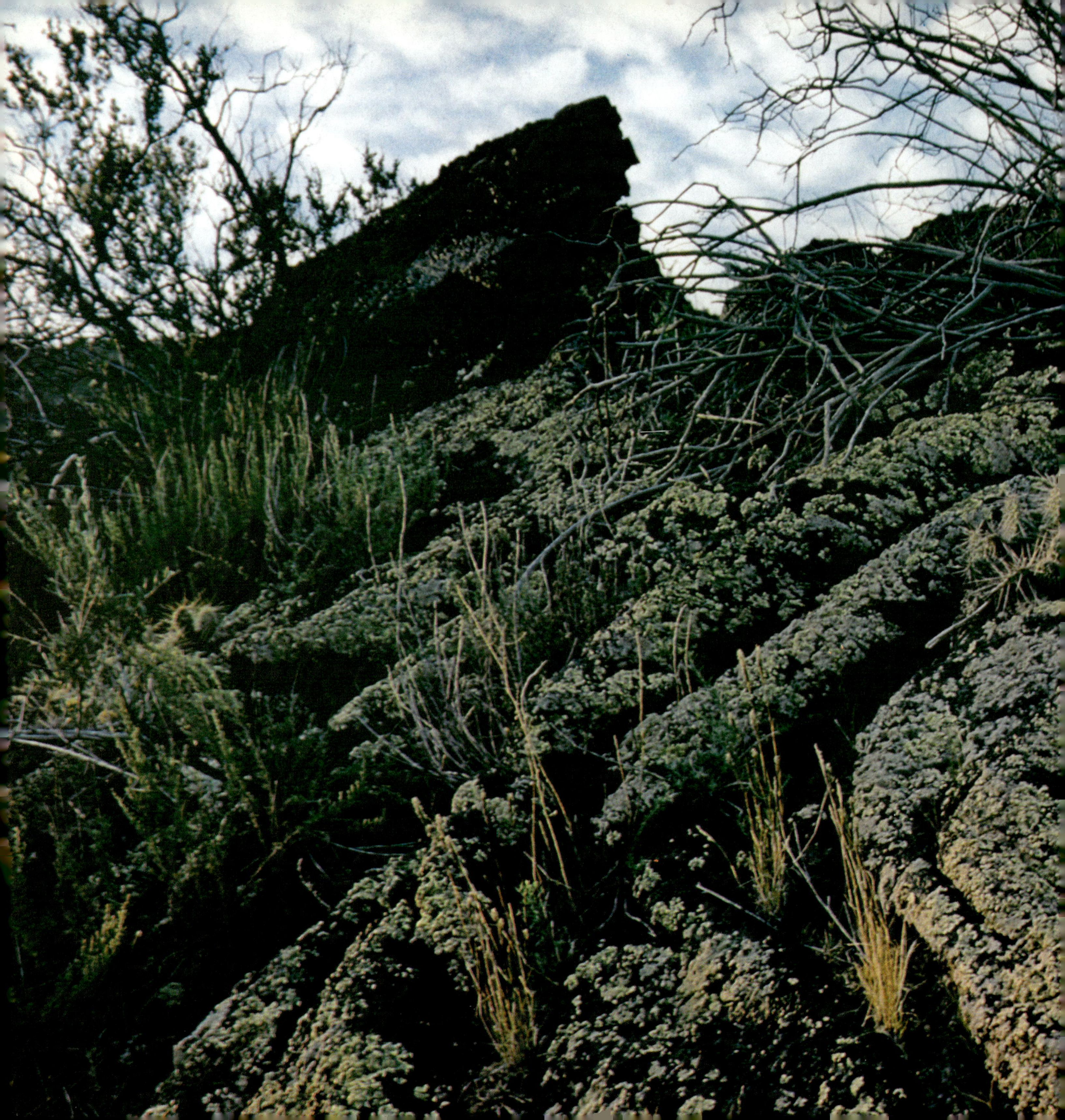

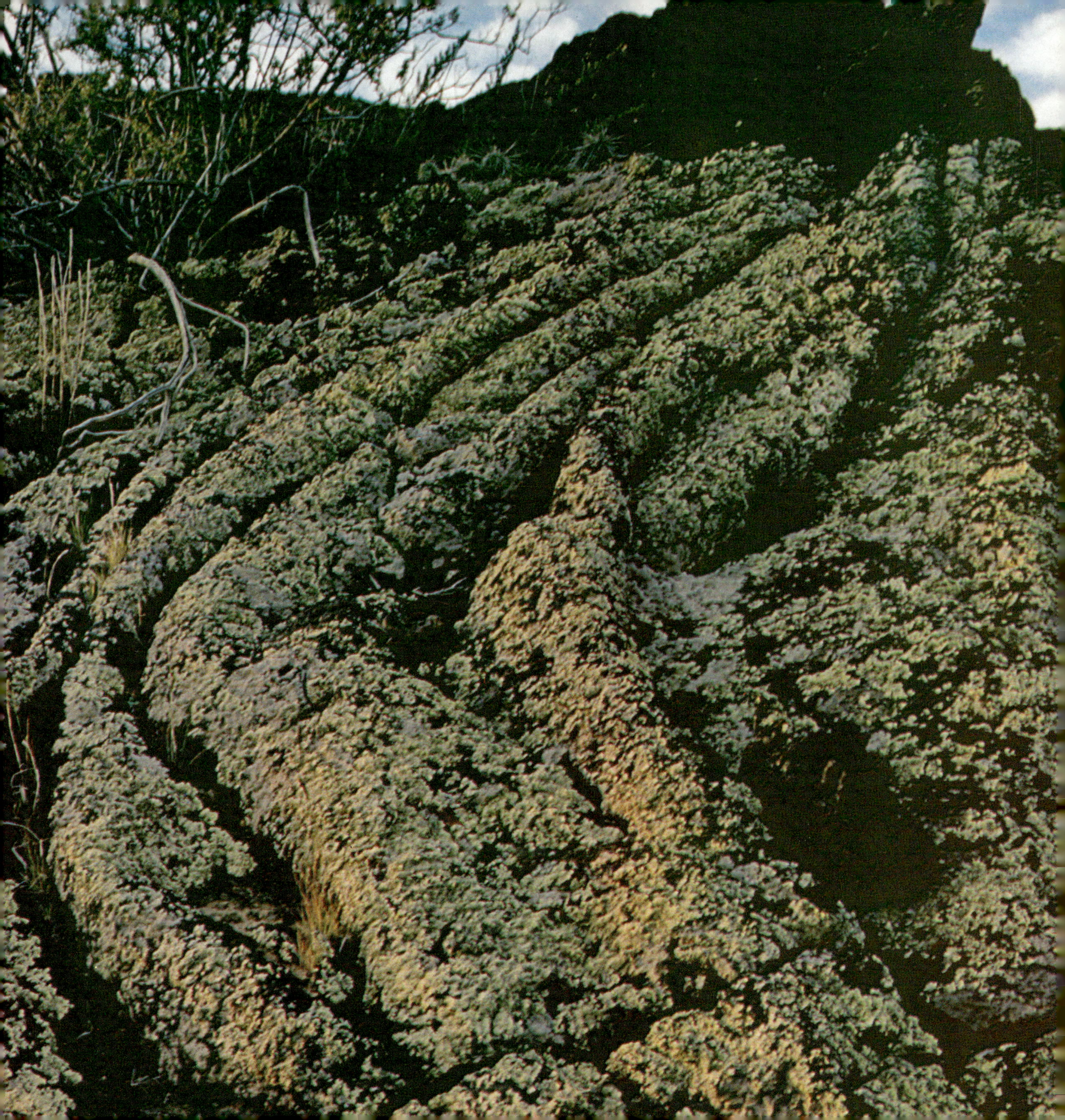

17

Coral pink sand dunes, Utah.

November 1970

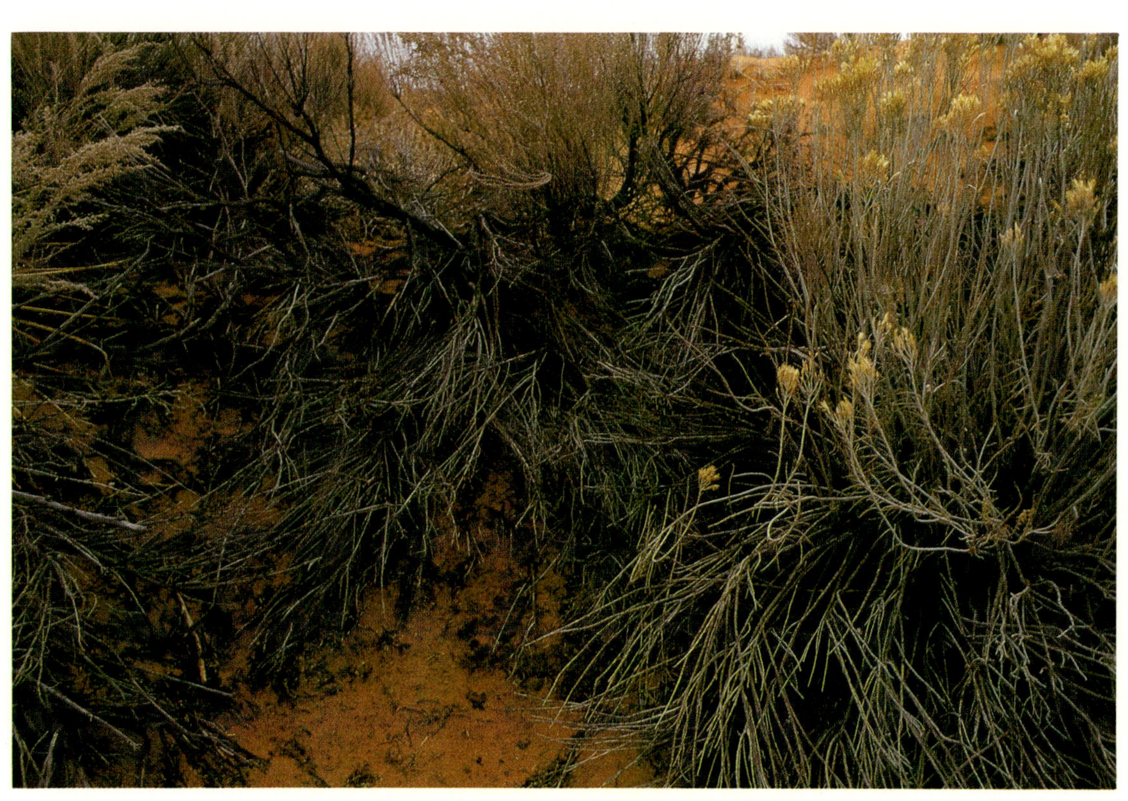

18
Valley of the Gods, Utah.
May 1971

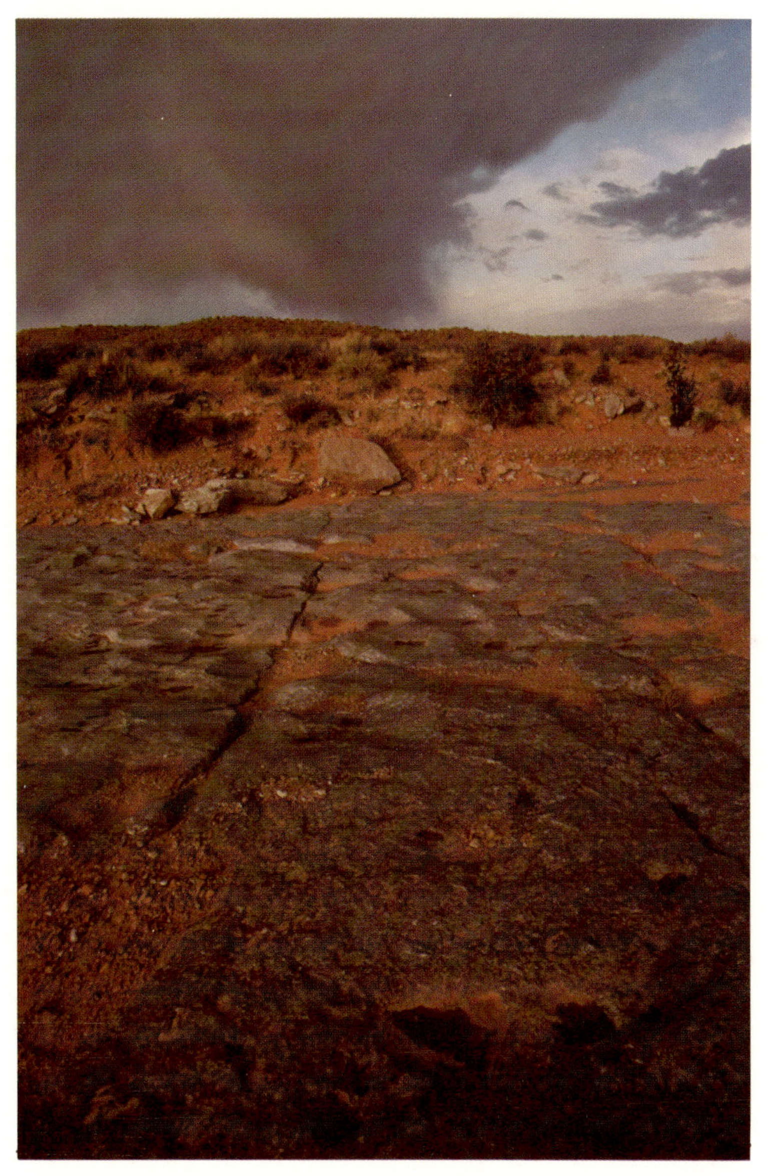

19
White Sands, New Mexico.
February 1971

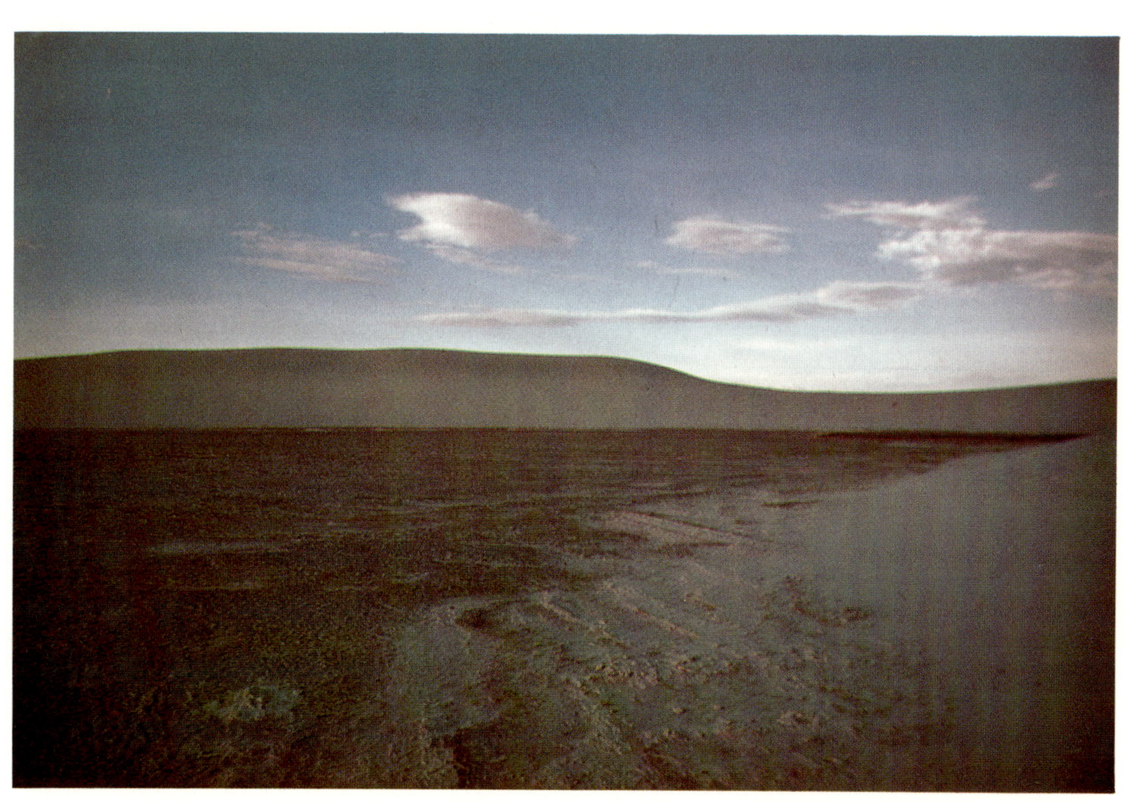

20

Mount Baboquivari, Arizona.
August 1972

From *Cactus Country,* a volume in the Time-Life Books series *The American Wilderness.*

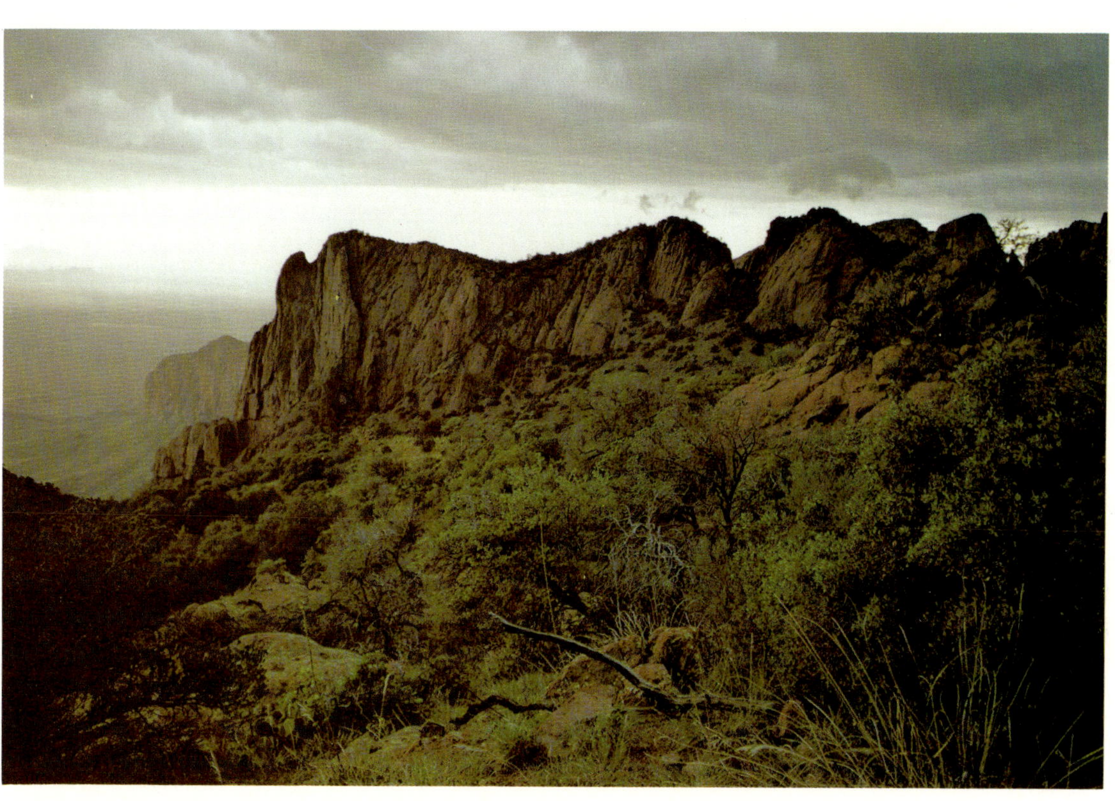

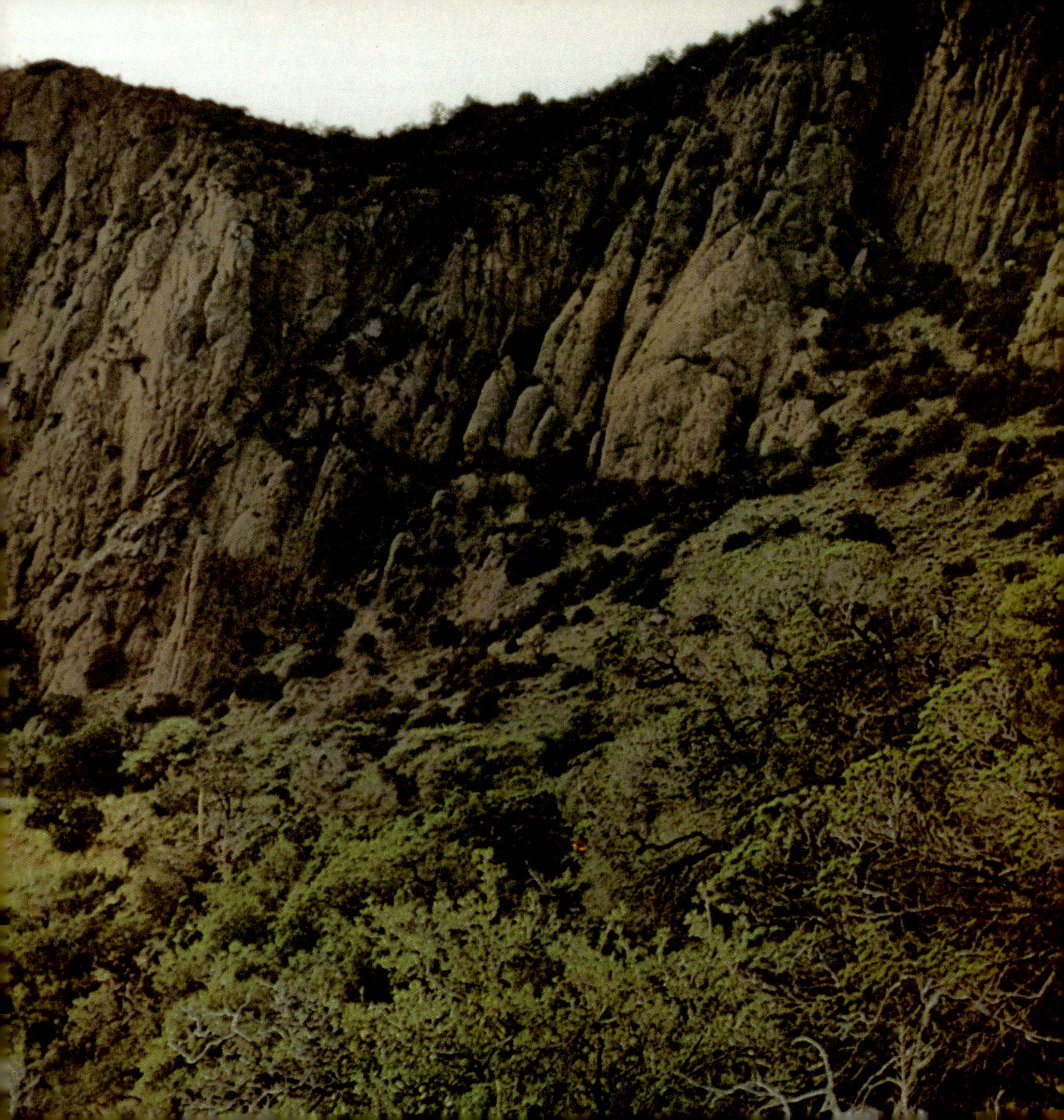

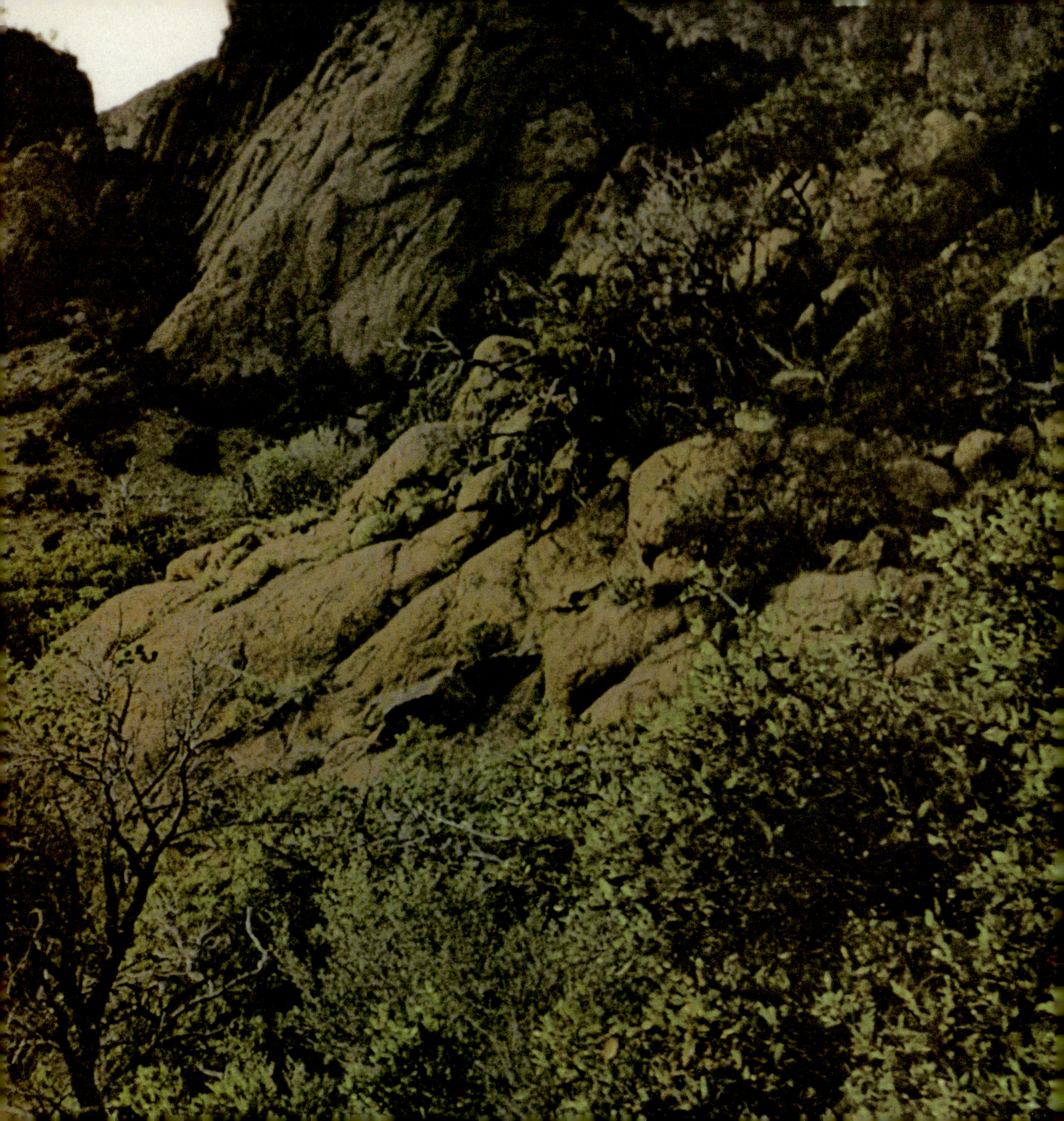

21

Kofa Mountains, Arizona.
August 1972

From *Cactus Country,* a volume in the Time-Life Books series *The American Wilderness.*

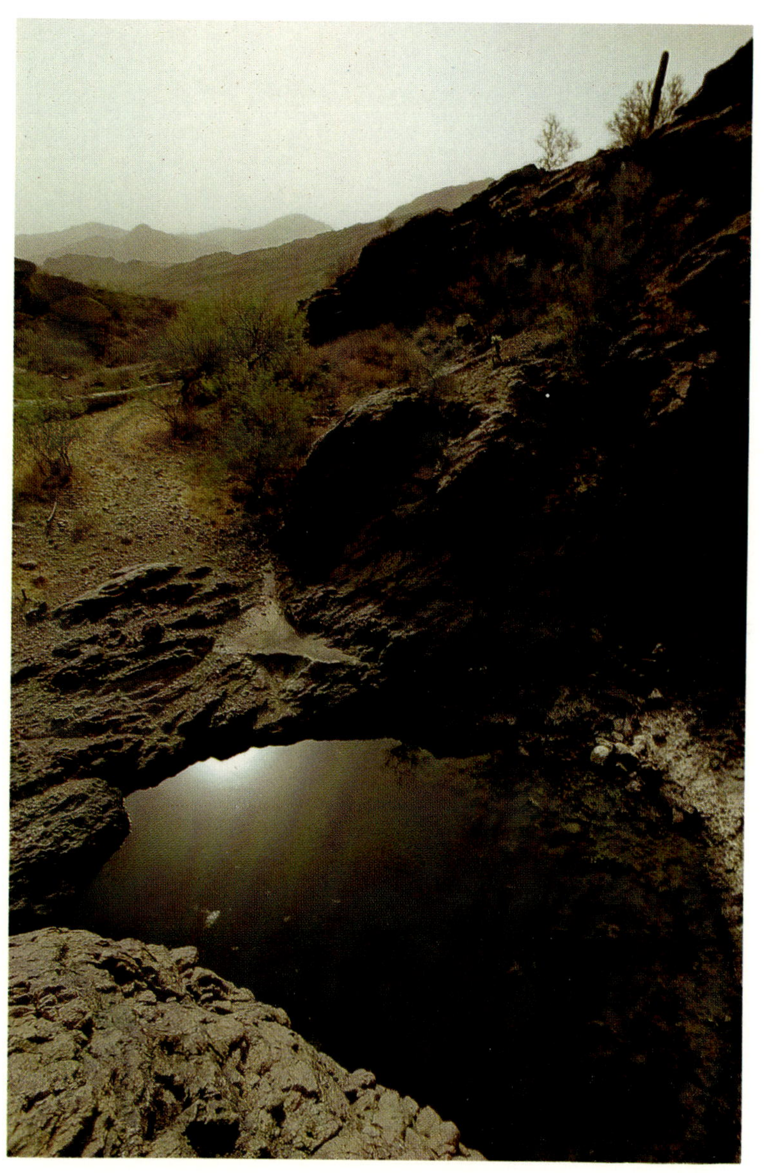

Alaska

22
Glacier Bay, Alaska.
The face of a glacier.
June 1971

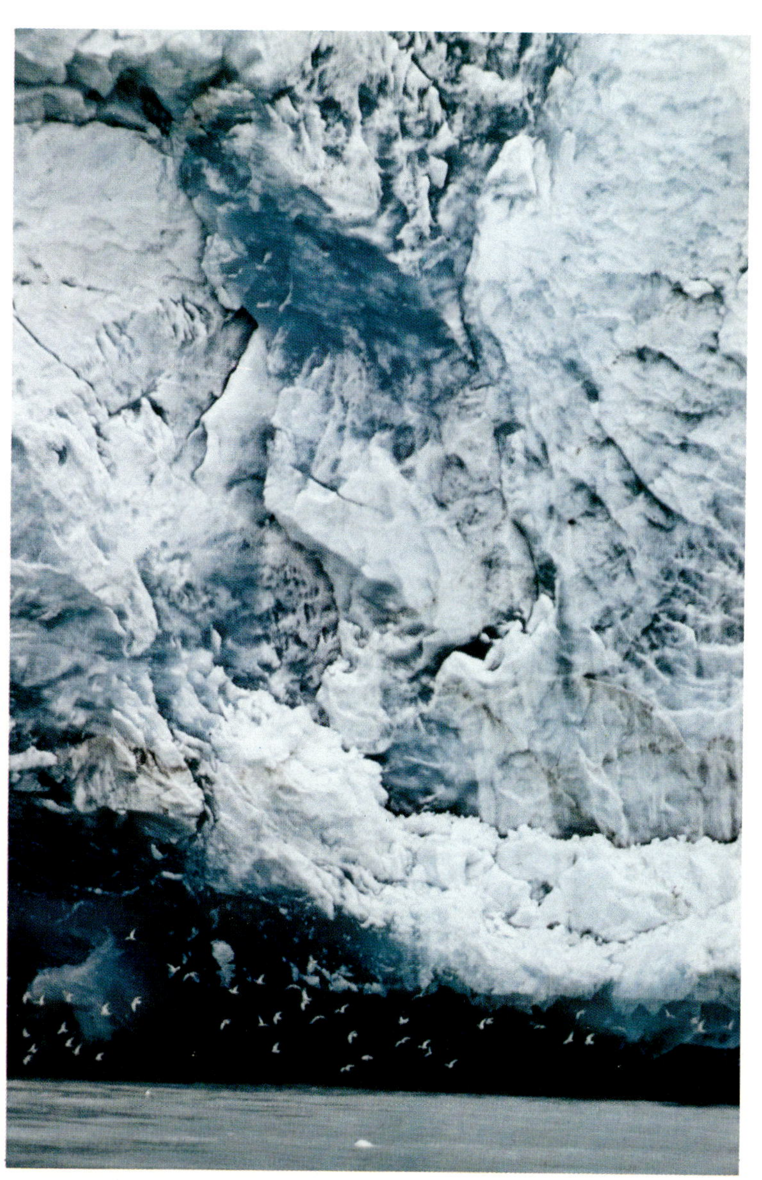

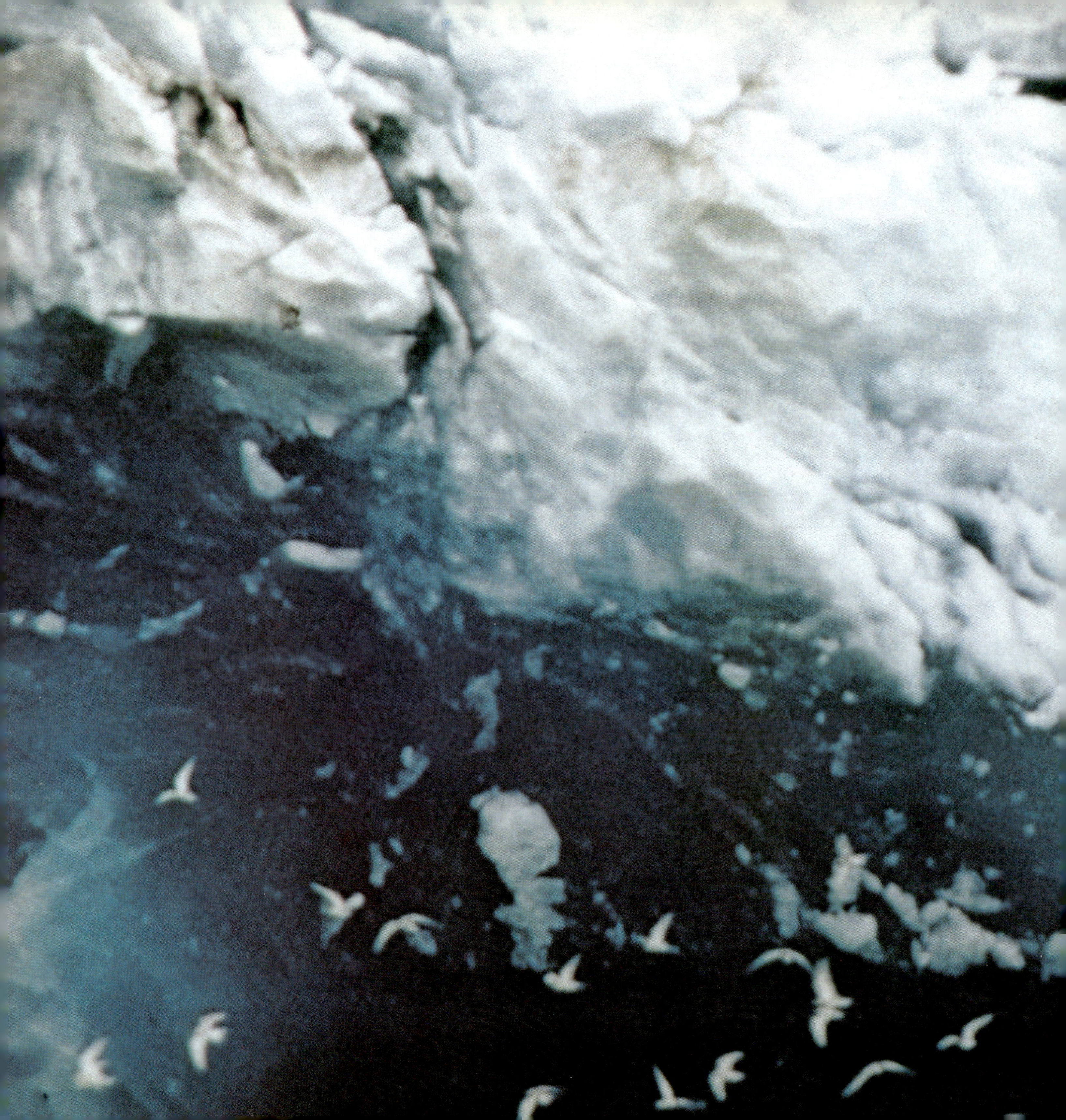

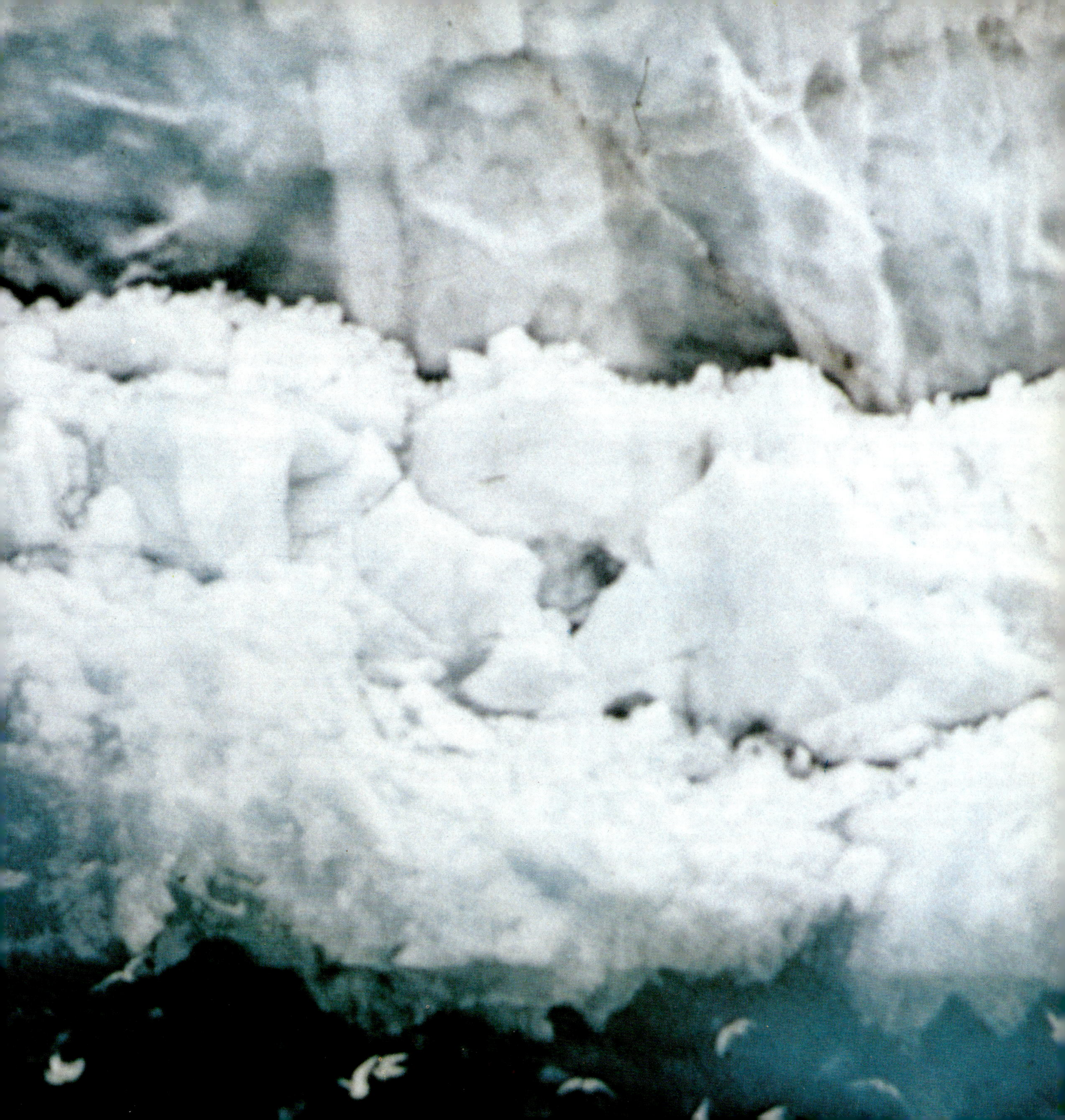

23

Glacier Bay, Alaska.

A diamond as big as the Ritz.

June 1971

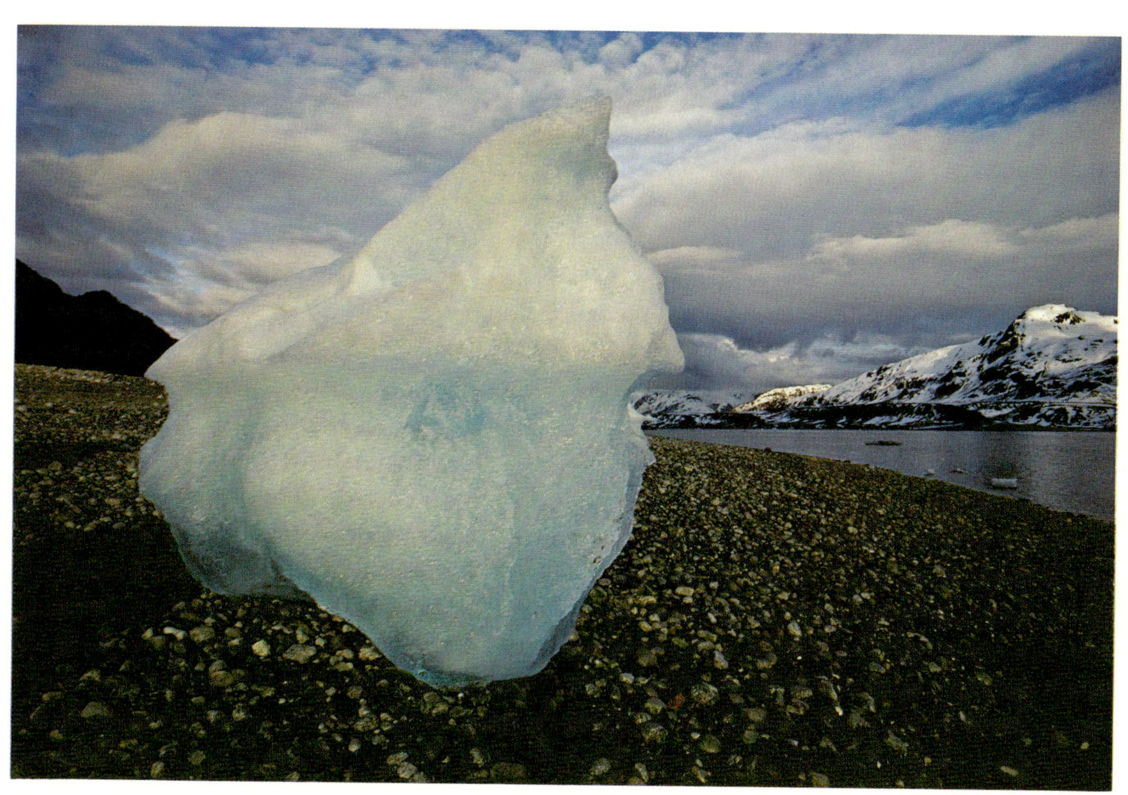

24
Glacier Bay, Alaska.
Fire and ice.
June 1971

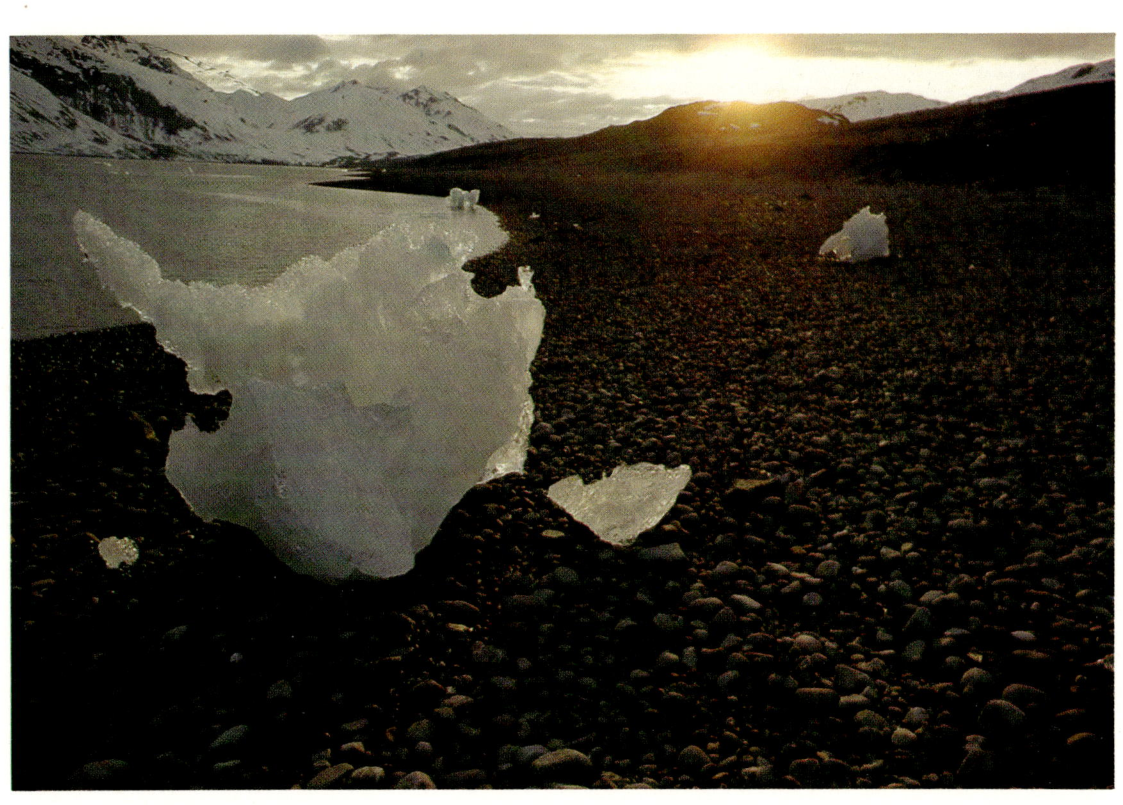

25
Glacier Bay, Alaska.
Icebergs.
June 1971

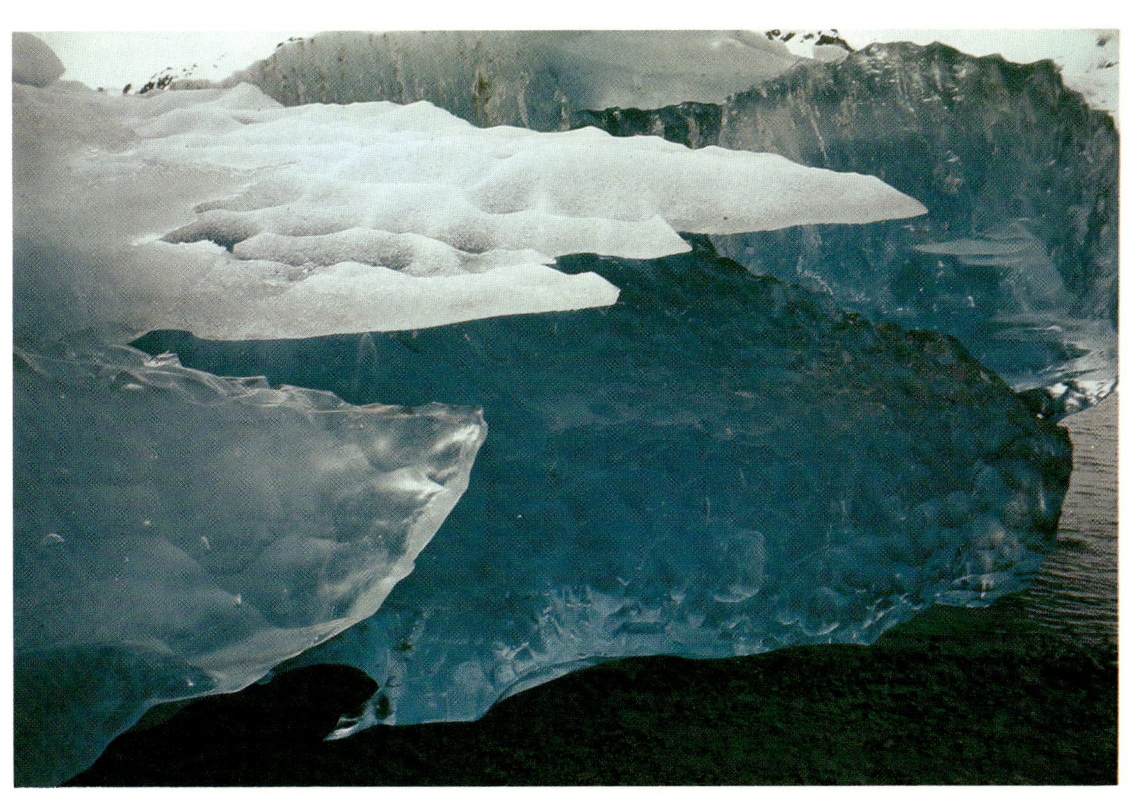

26
Glacier Bay, Alaska.
After the bear.
June 1971

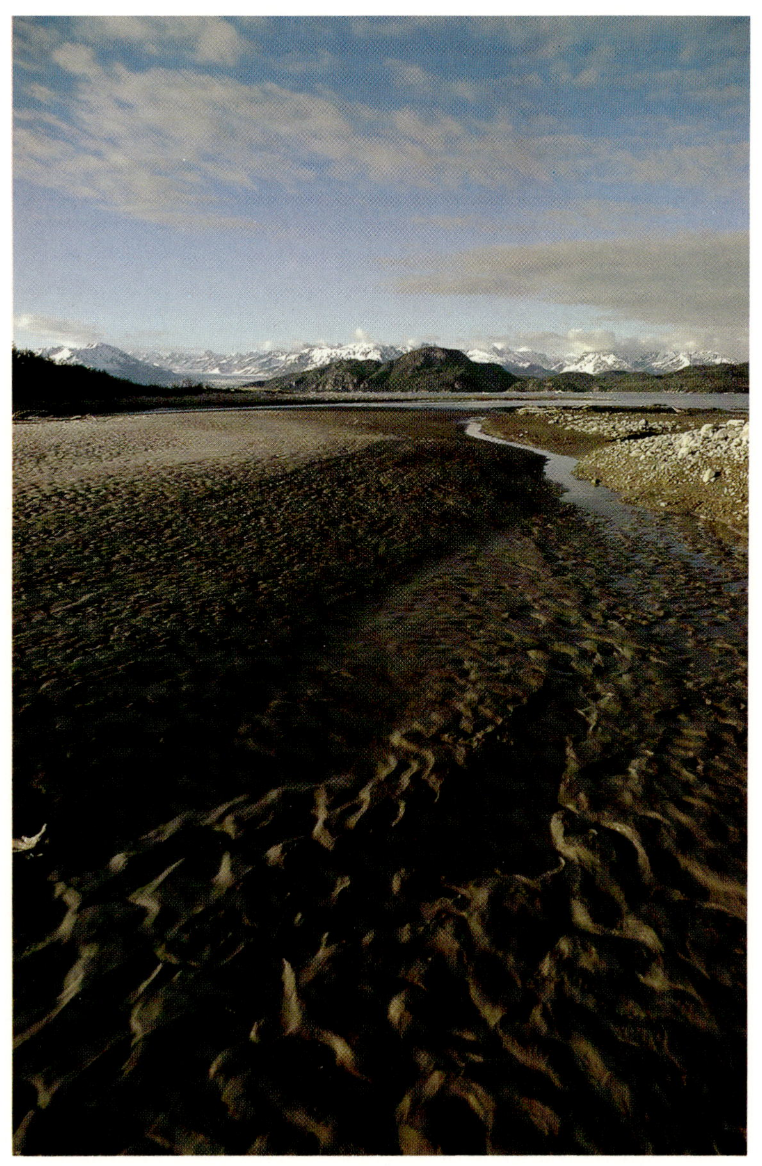

27
Glacier Bay, Alaska.
Blackwater Pond.
June 1971

From *Wild Alaska,* a volume in the Time-Life Books series *The American Wilderness.*

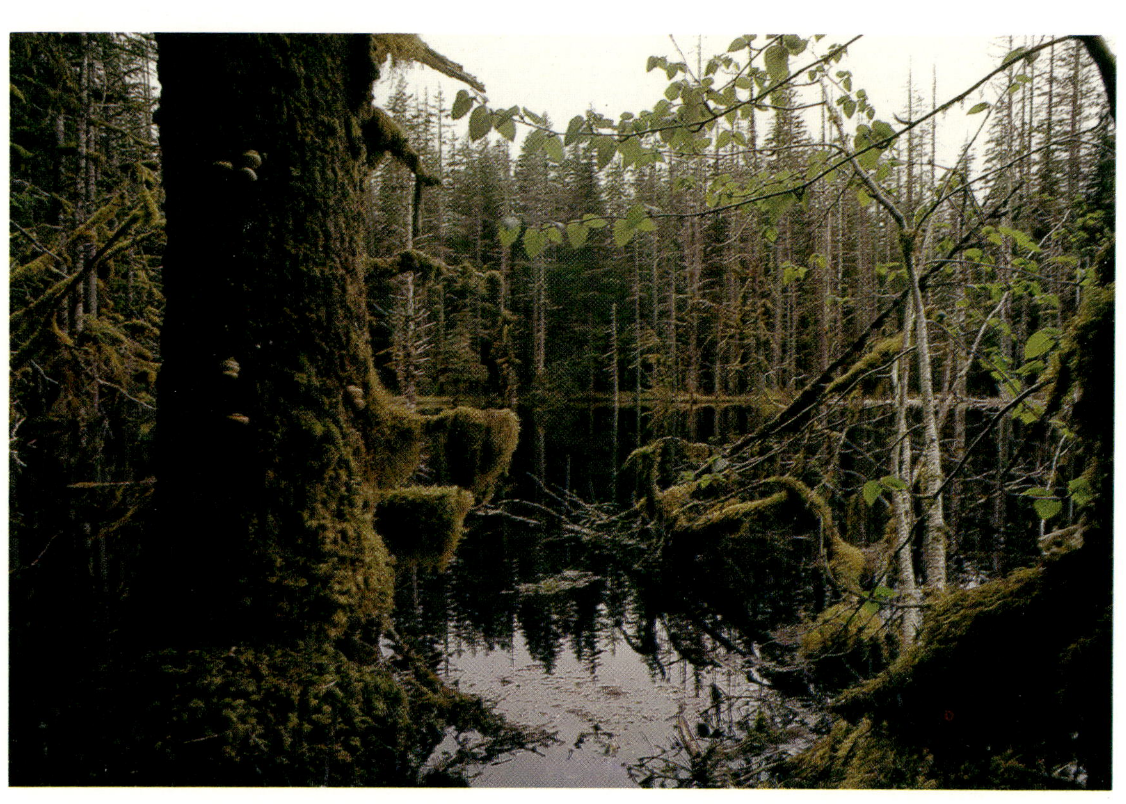

28
Glacier Bay, Alaska.
Bartlett Cove.
June 1971

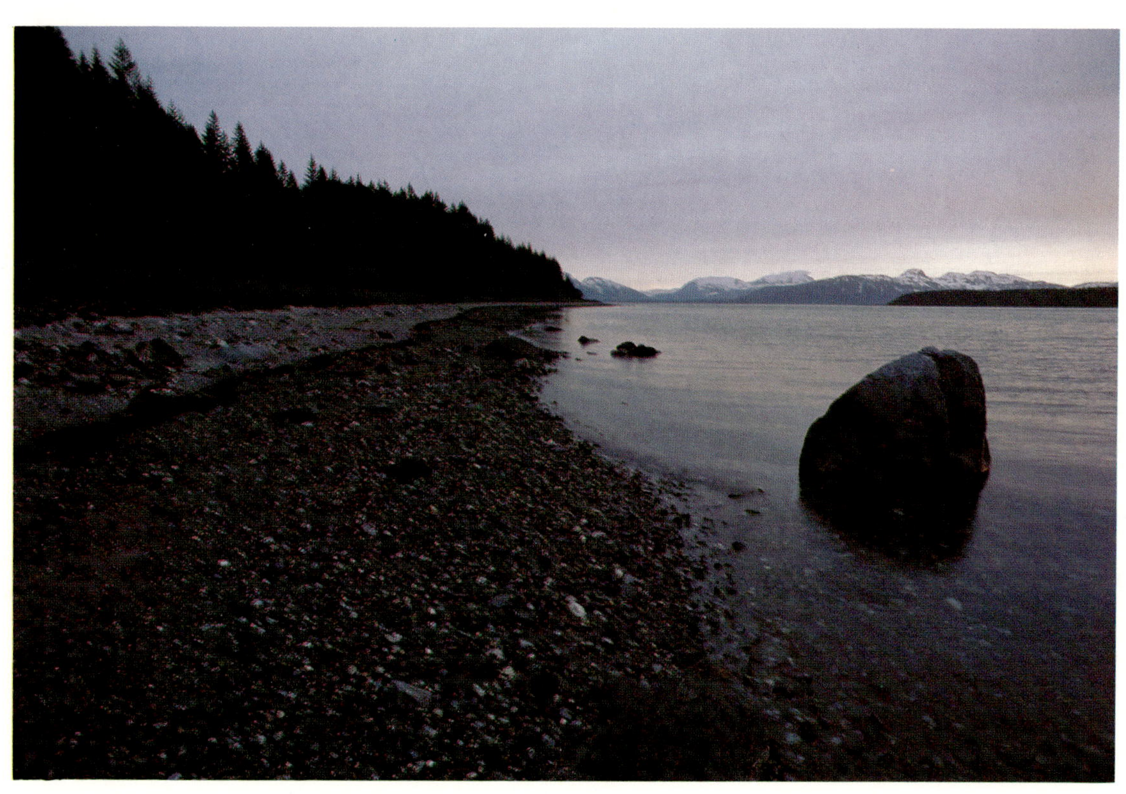

29
Denali, Alaska.
Wild roses.
July 1971

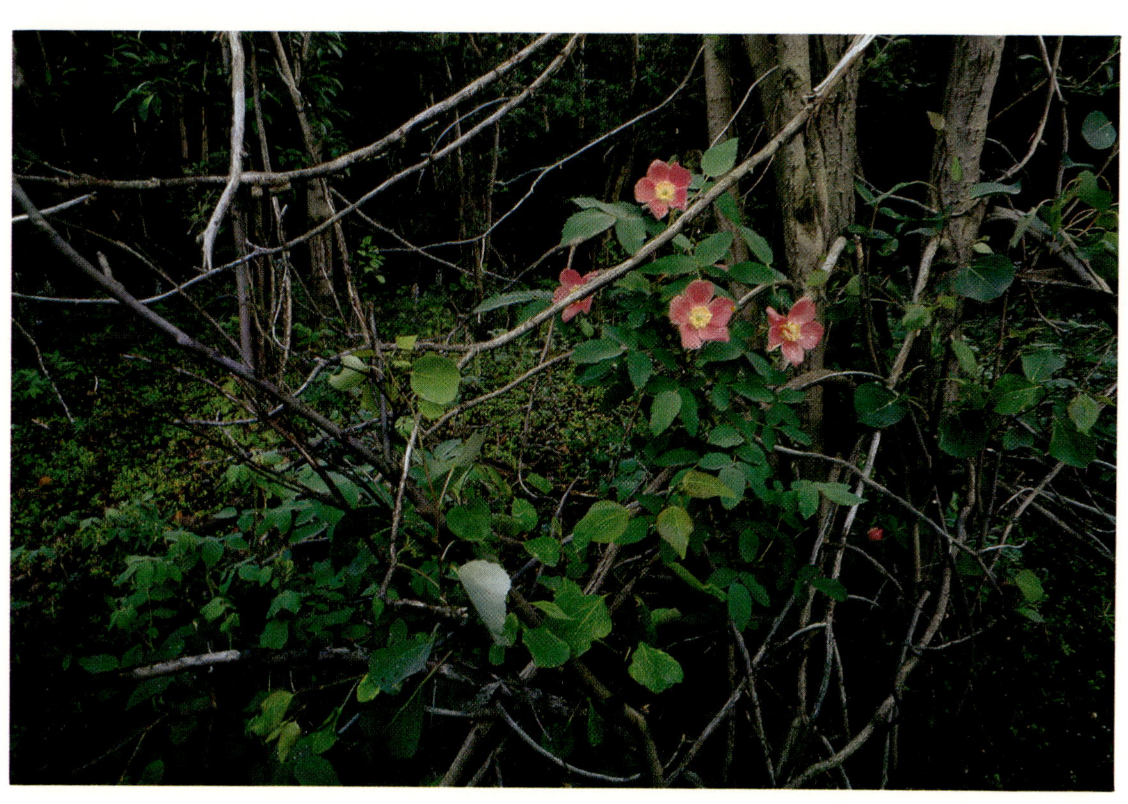

30
Denali, Alaska.
Fox.
July 1971

From *Wild Alaska,* a volume in the Time-Life Books series *The American Wilderness.*

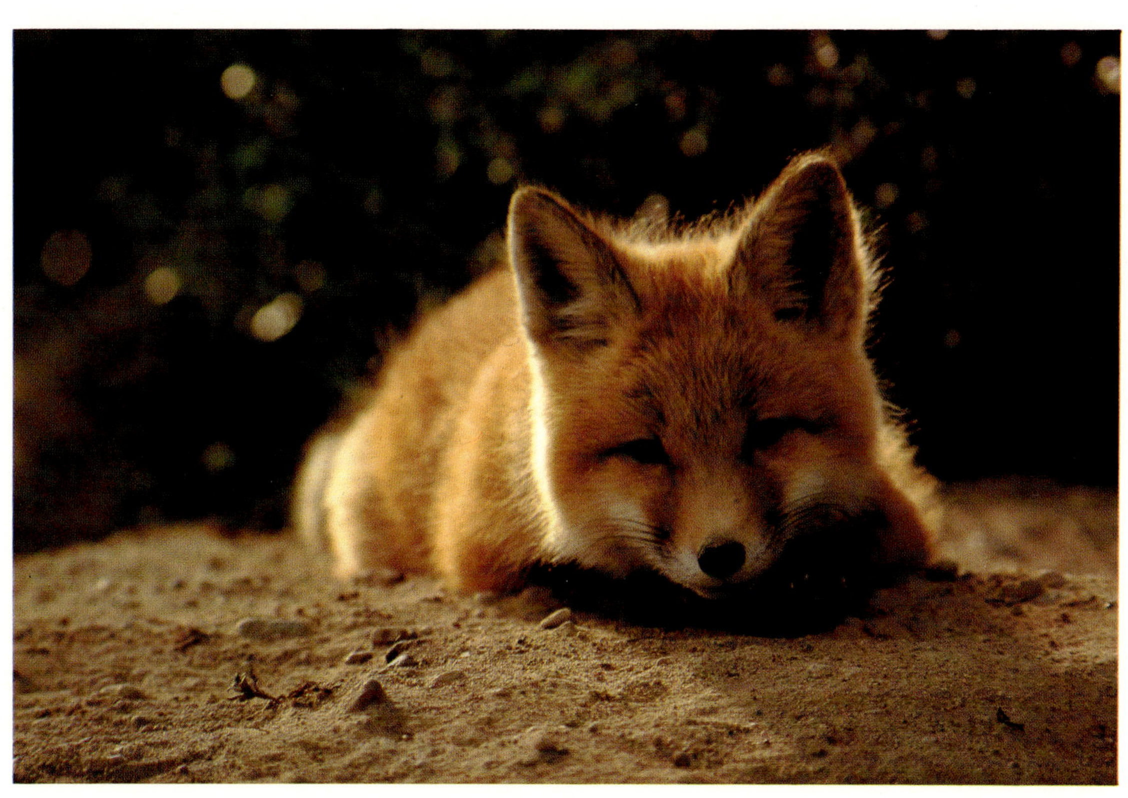

31
Denali, Alaska.
Sunset.
July 1971

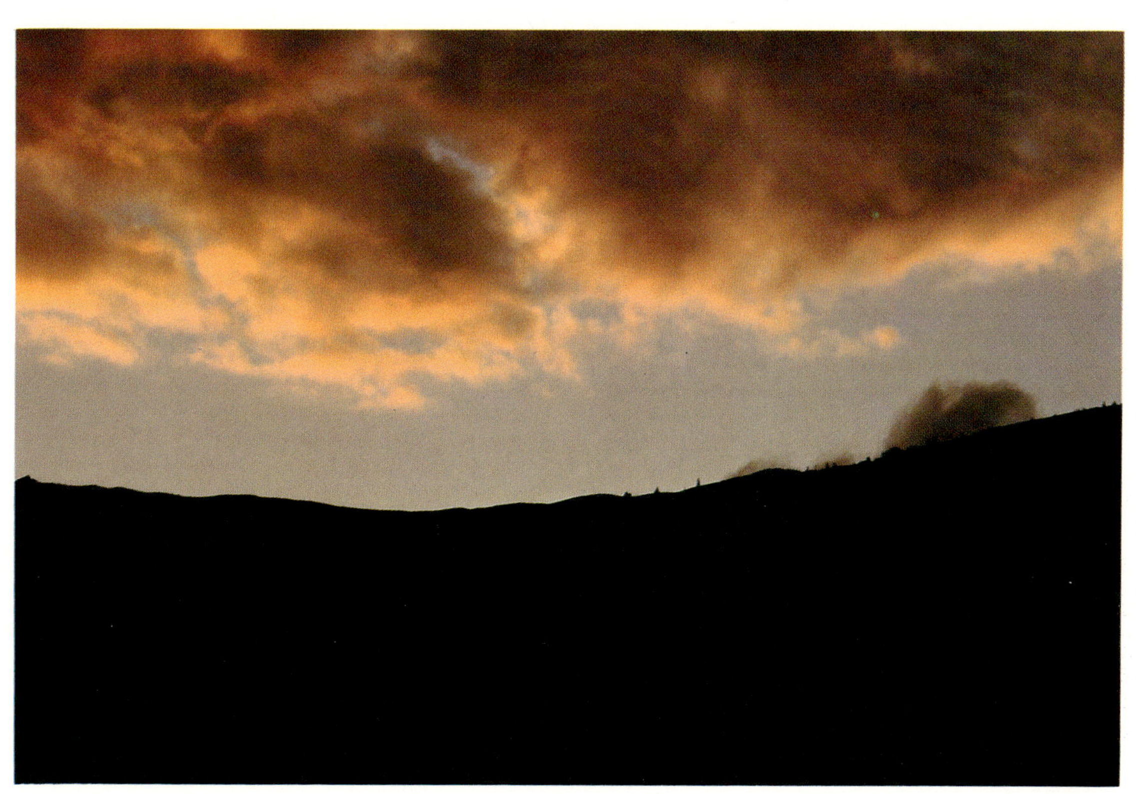

32
North Slope, Alaska.
July 1971

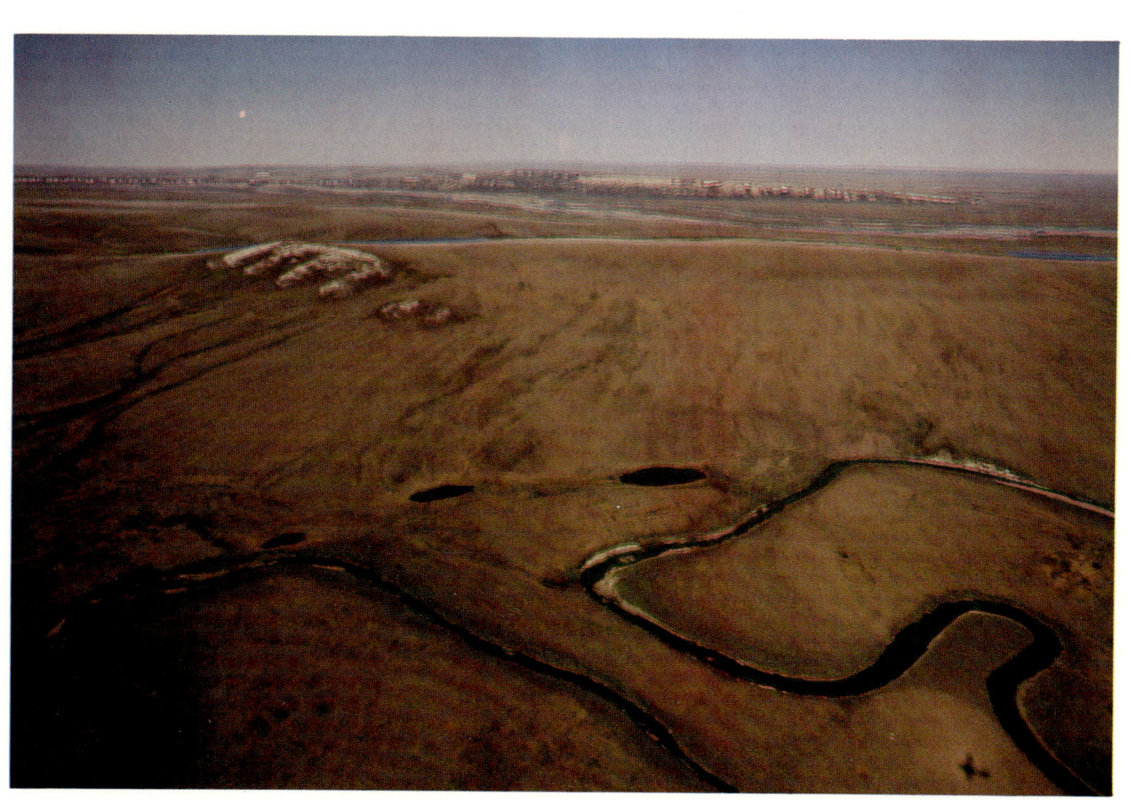

33

Katmai, Alaska.

The Valley of Ten Thousand Smokes.

July 1971

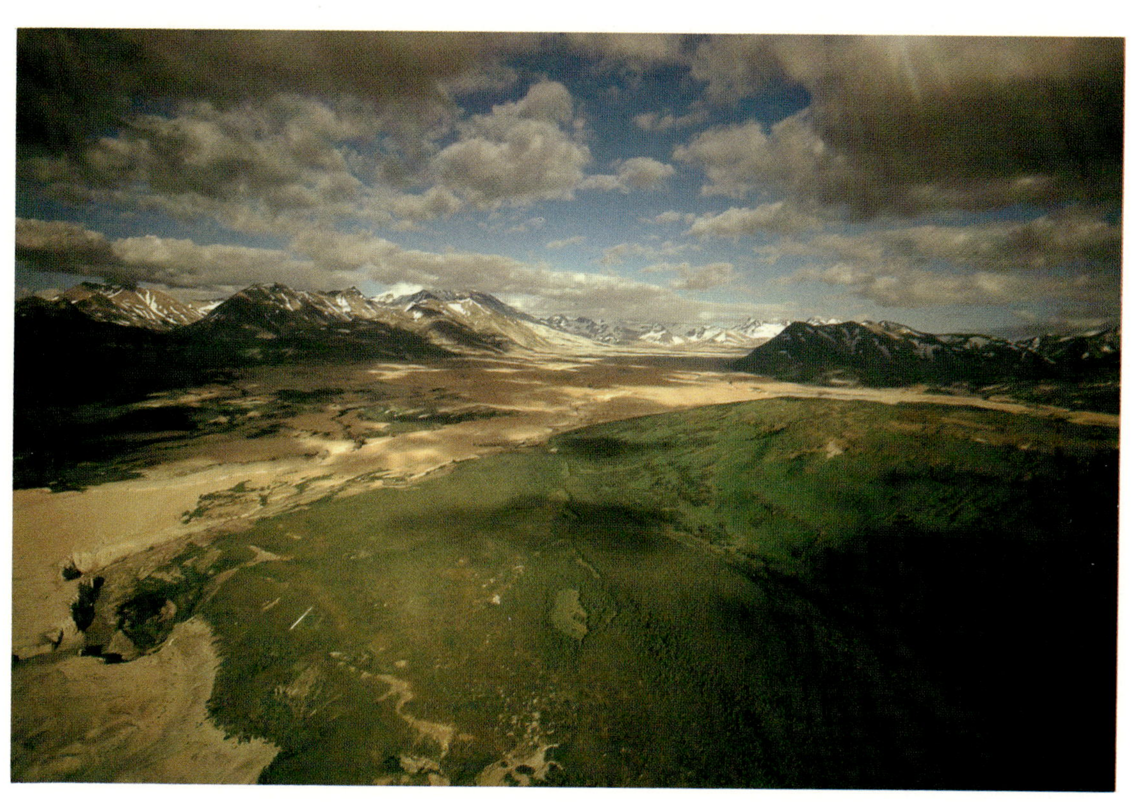

34

Katmai, Alaska.

Snow on the mountain.

July 1971

From *Wild Alaska,* a volume in the Time-Life Books series *The American Wilderness.*

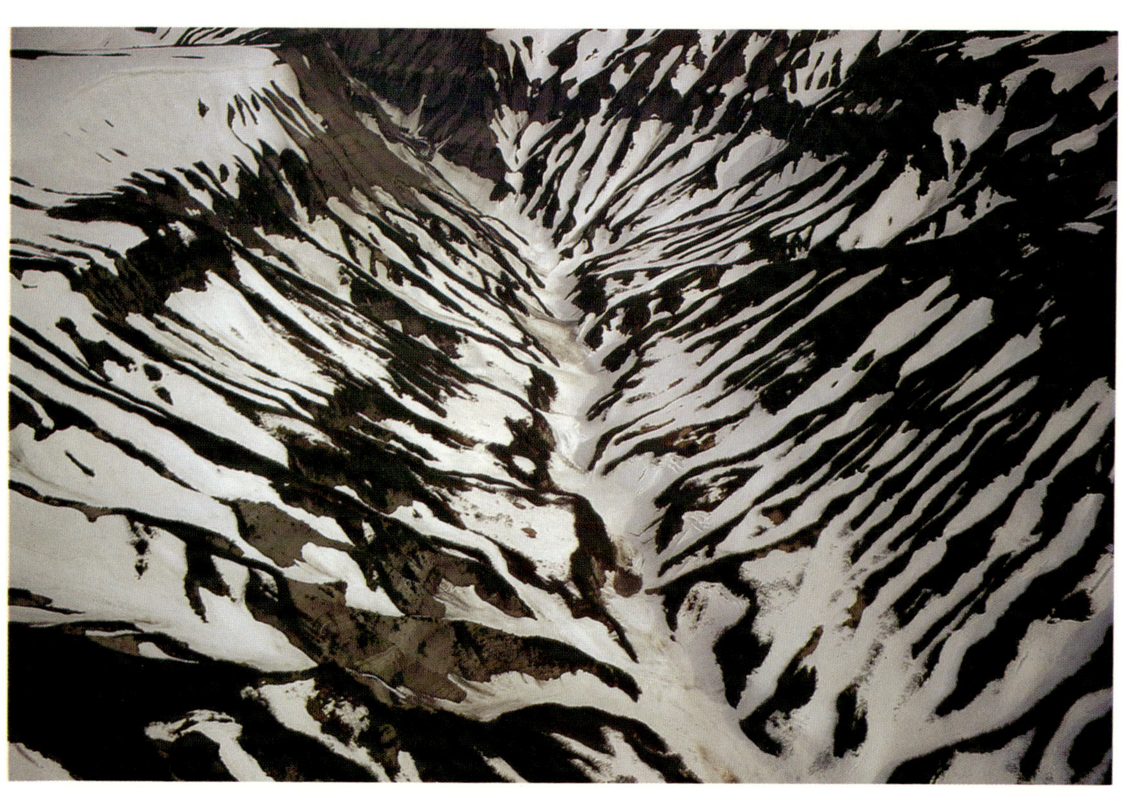

Texas

35
Hill Country, Texas.
LBJ Ranch. Wild flowers.
June 1972

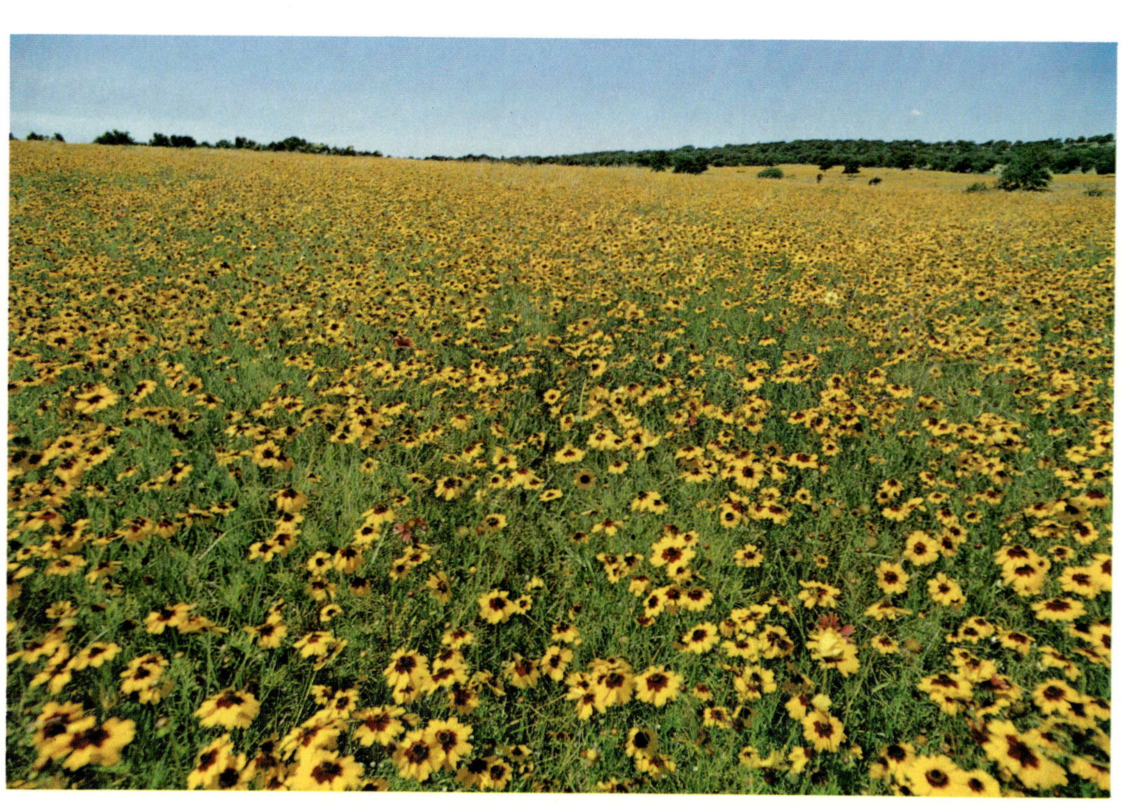

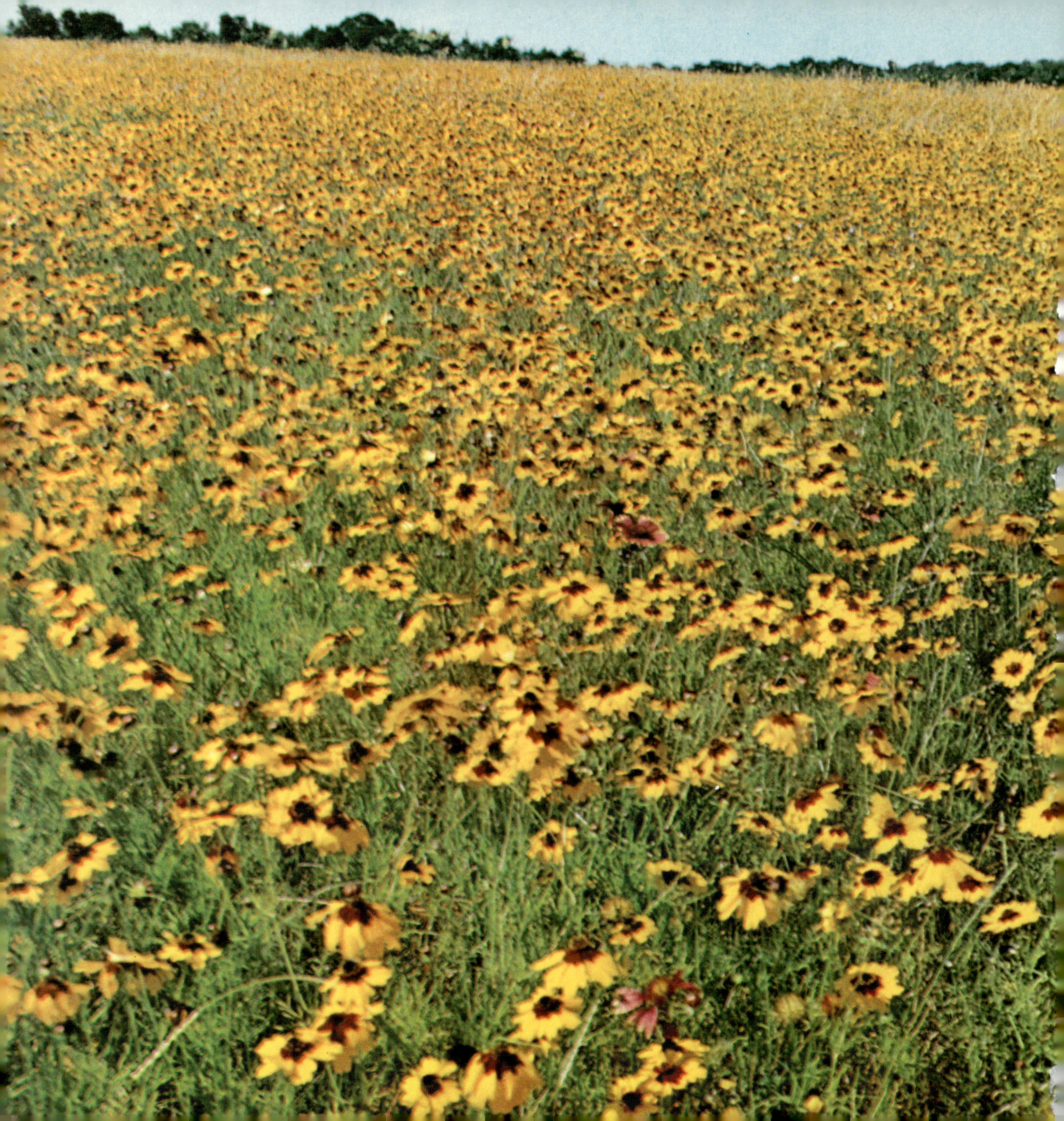

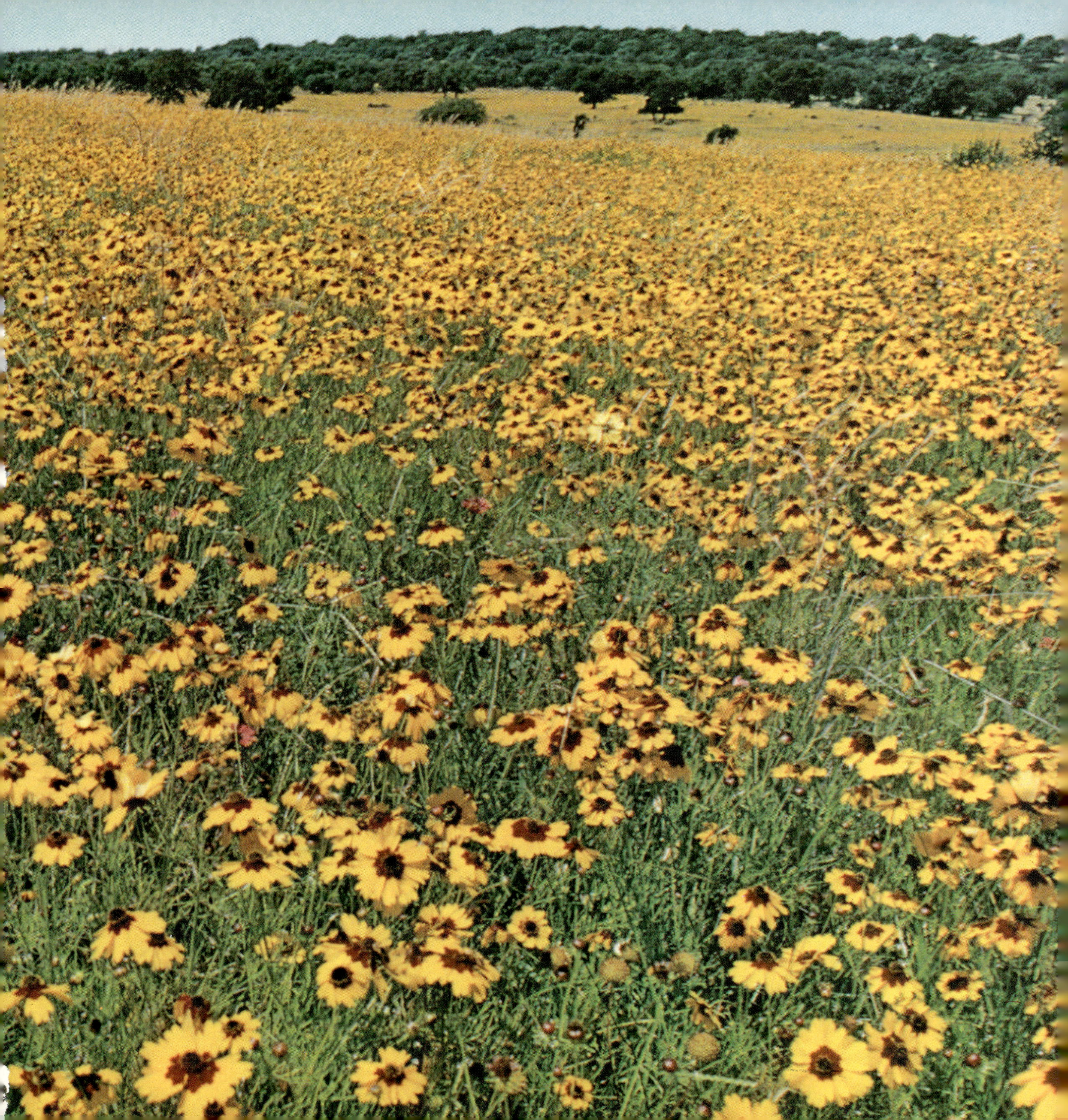

36

Hill Country, Texas.

LBJ Ranch. Danz in the evening.

May 1973

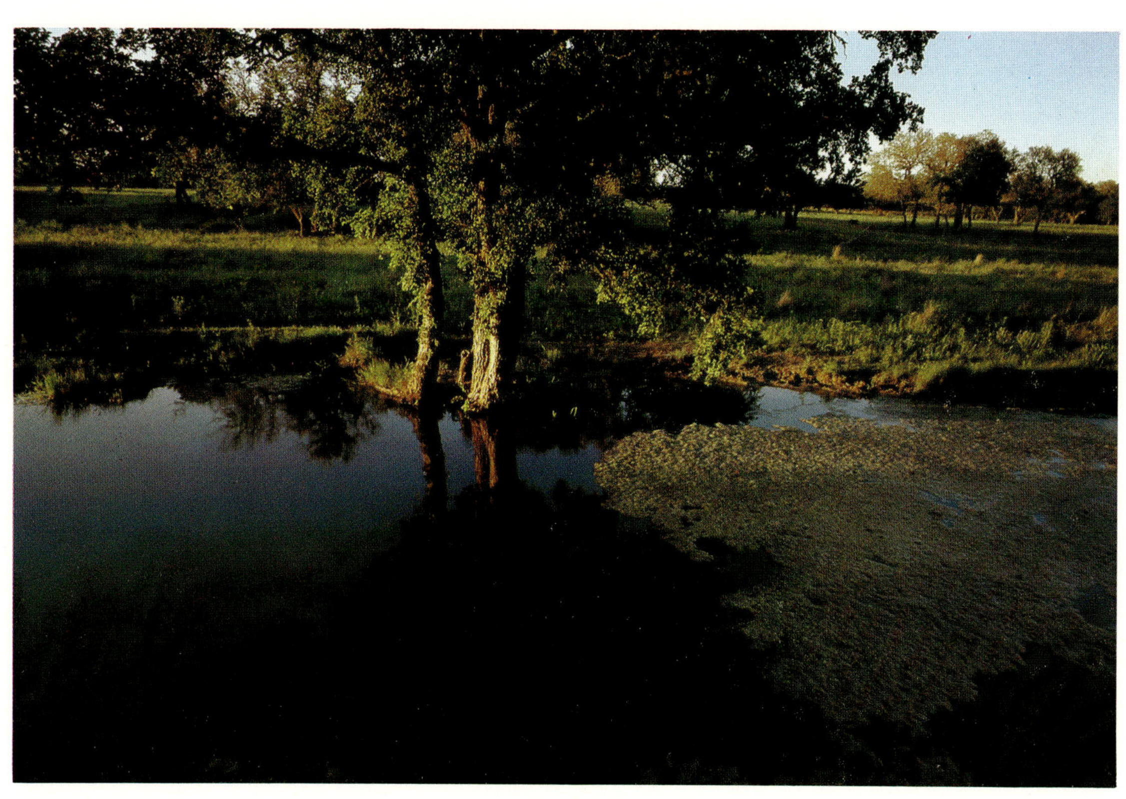

37
Hill Country, Texas.
The Pedernales.
May 1973

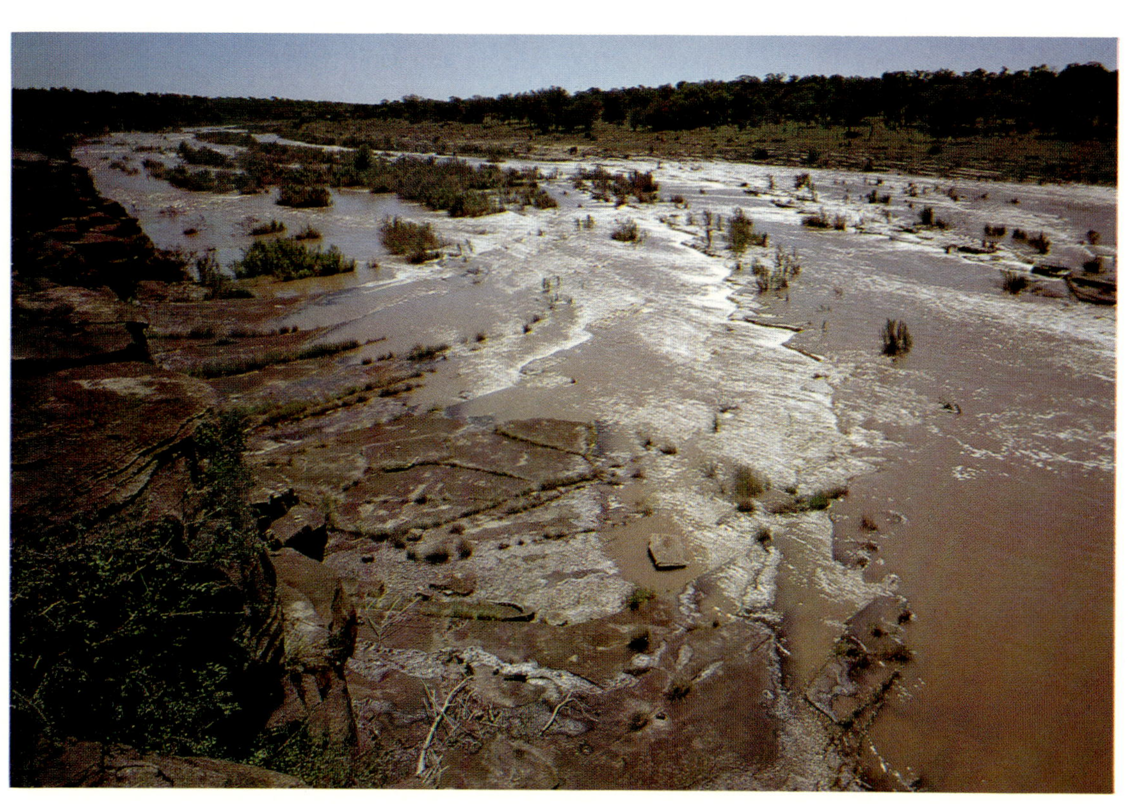

38
Hill Country, Texas.
Indian paintbrush.
May 1973

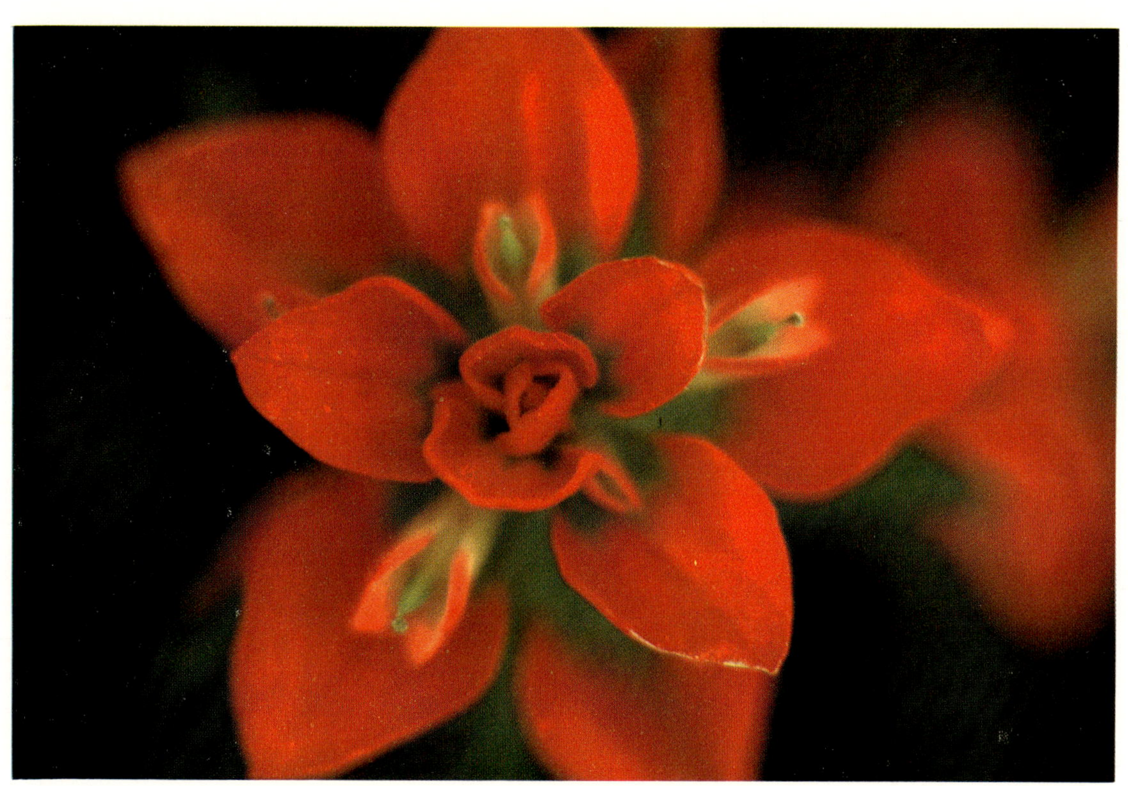

39
Hill Country, Texas.
LBJ Ranch. Longhorn bull.
May 1973

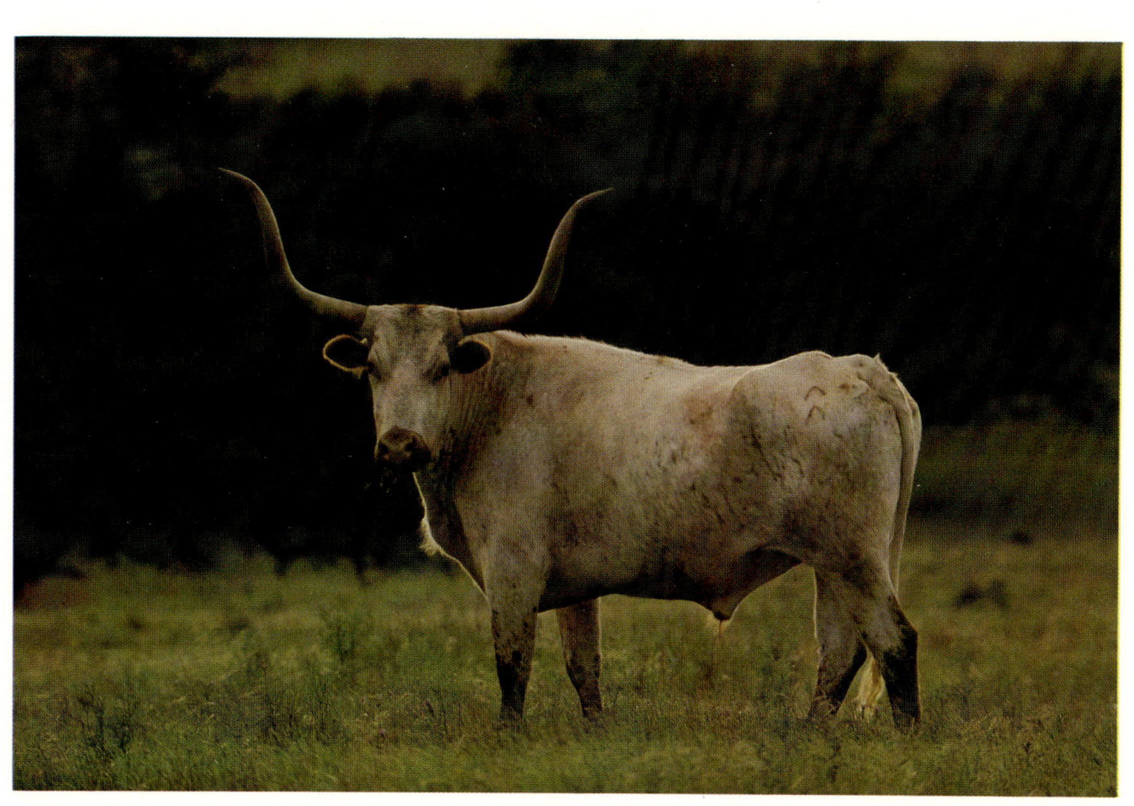

New England

40
Harriman State Park, New York.
Popolopen Gorge Trail.
December 1972

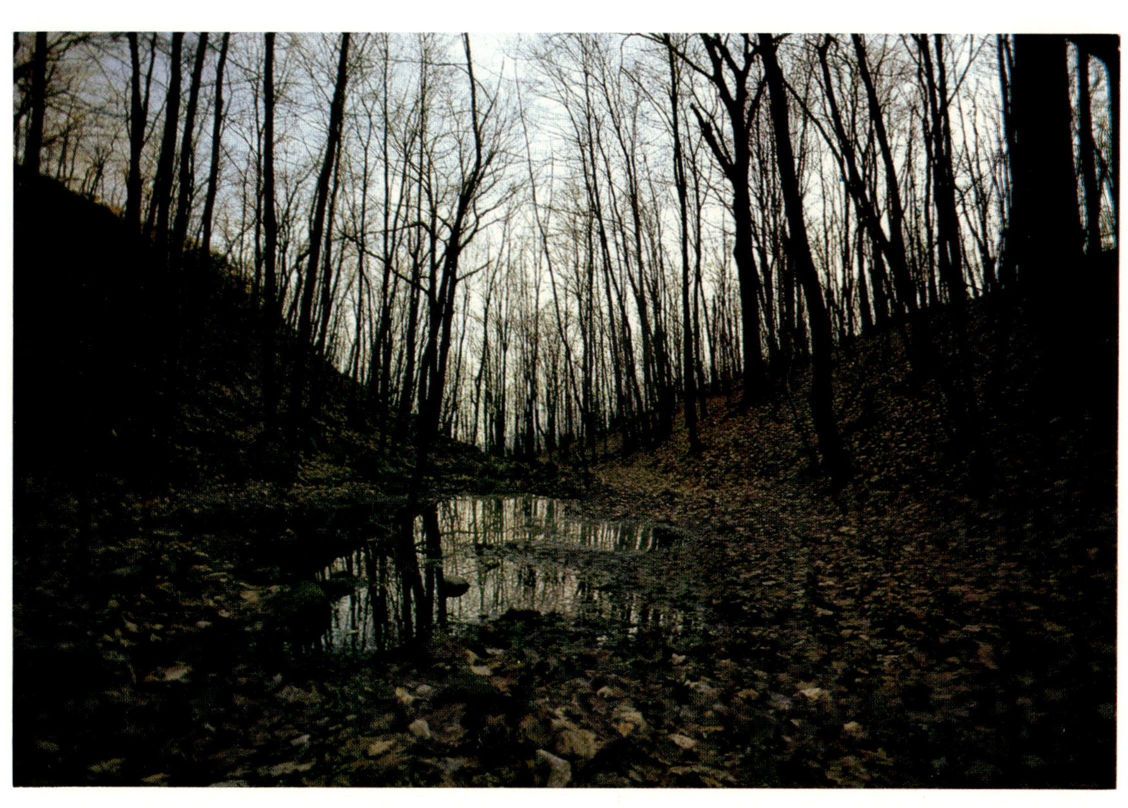

41
Harriman State Park, New York.
Turkey Hill Lake.
January 1973

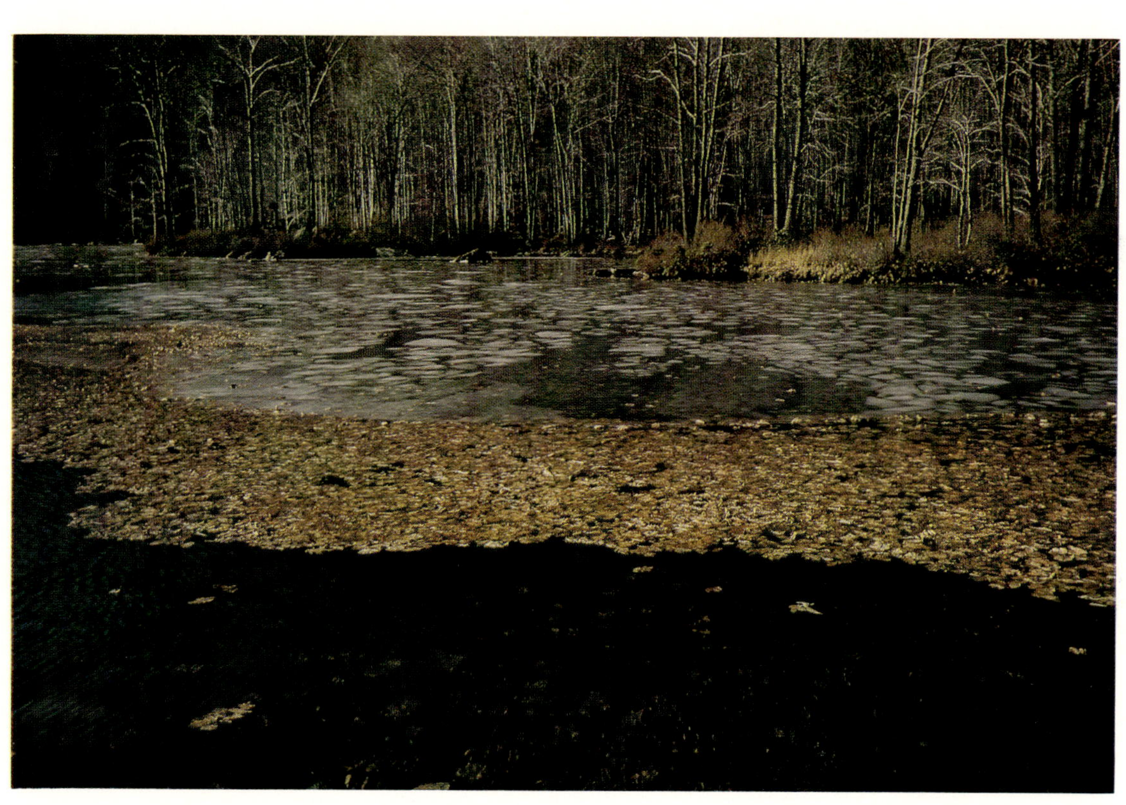

42
Harriman State Park, New York.
Long Mountain.
January 1973

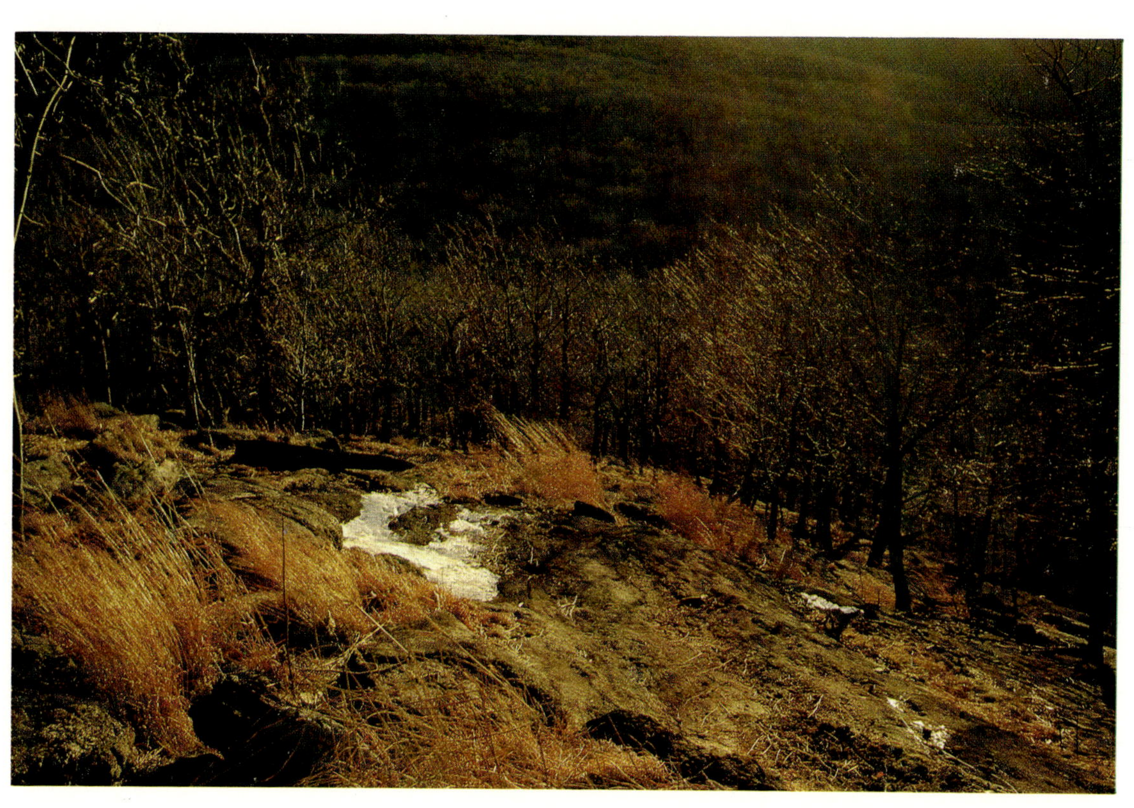

43

Harriman State Park, New York.

Red Cross Trail.

January 1973

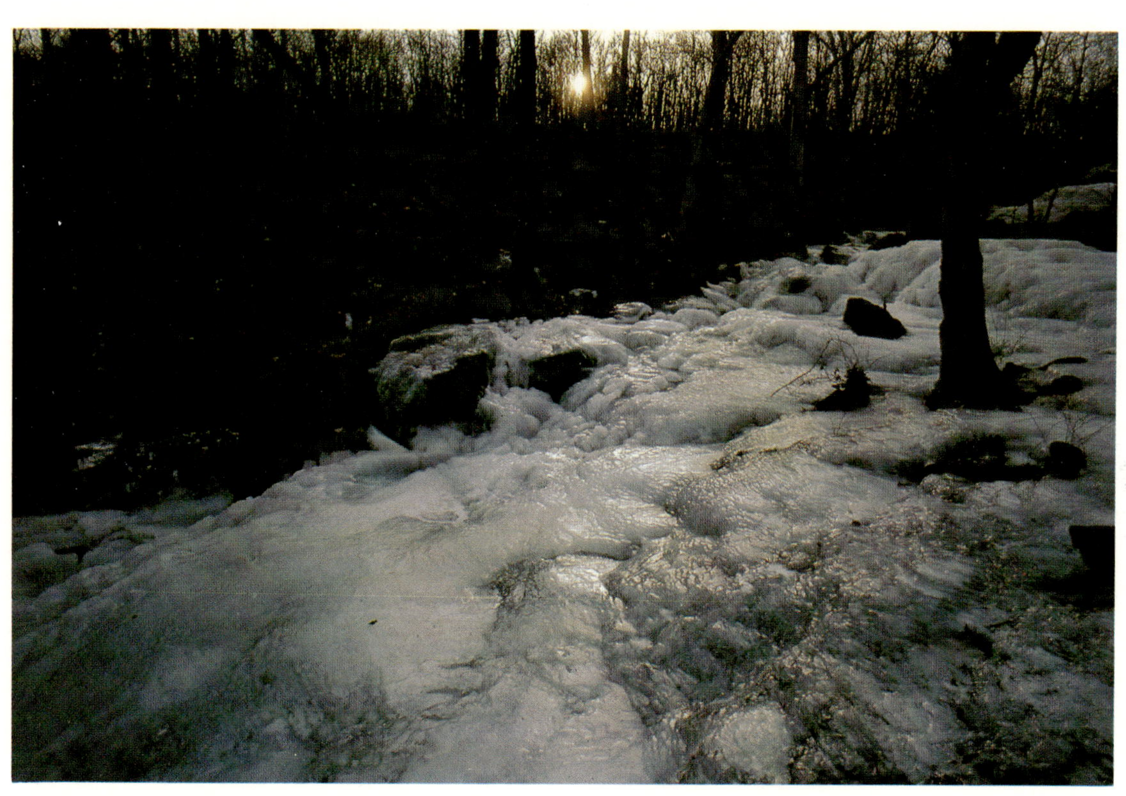

44

Harriman State Park, New York.

Ice day.

December 1972

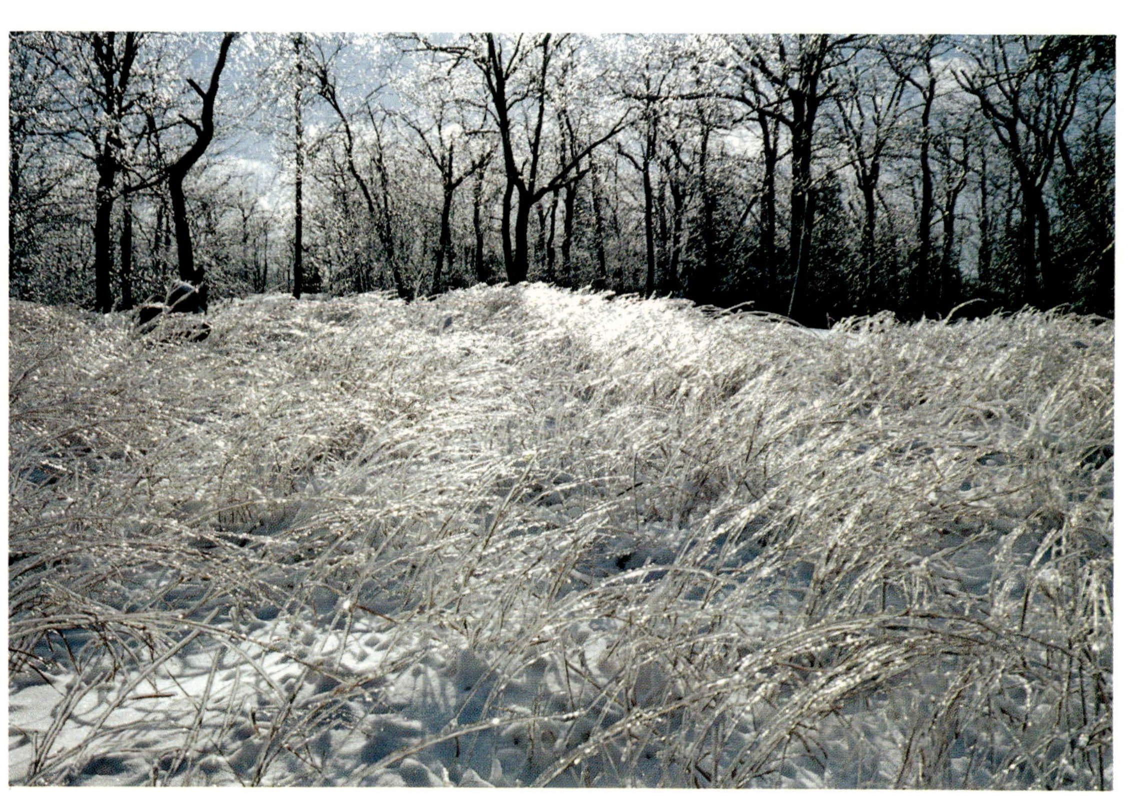

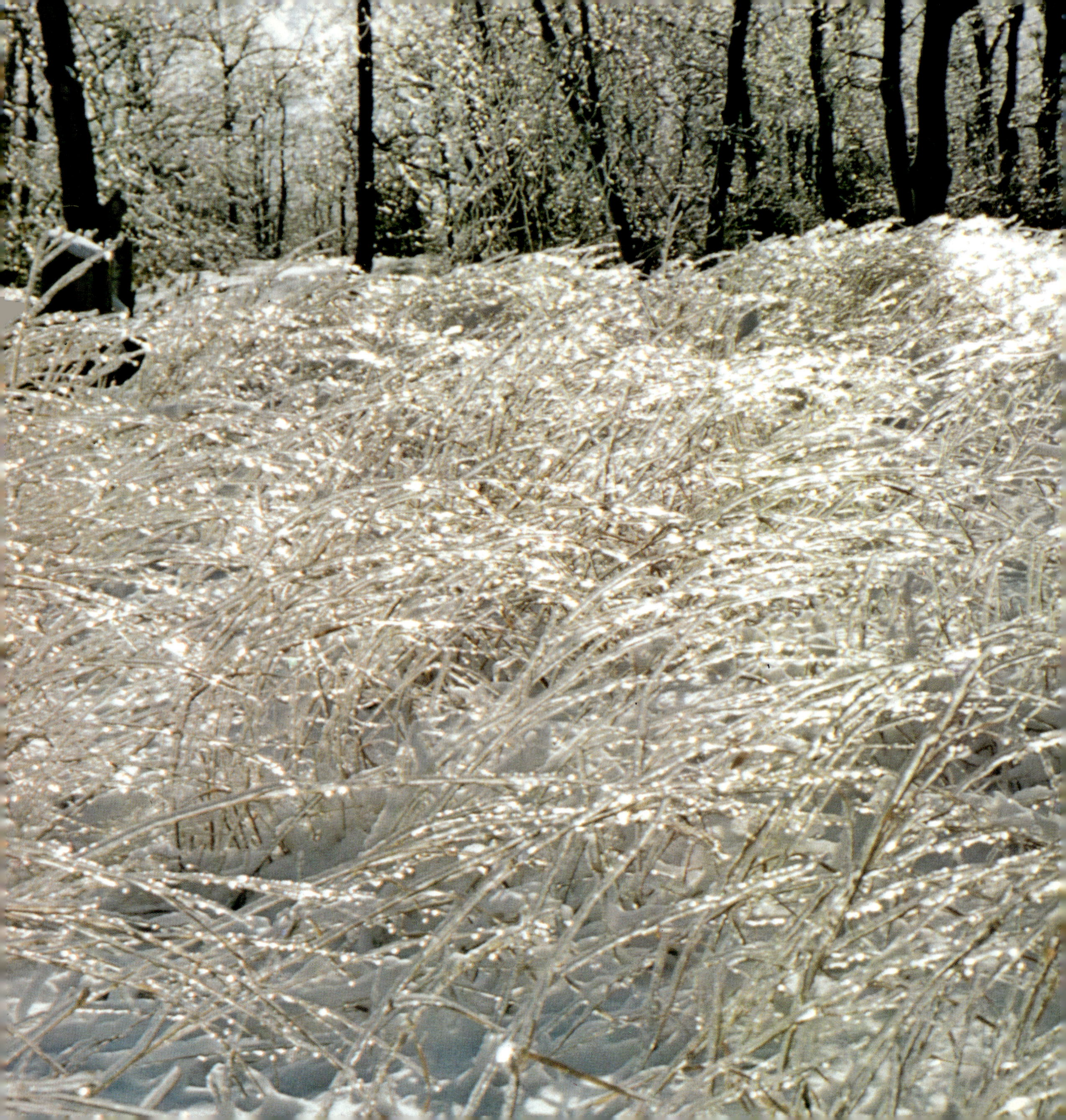

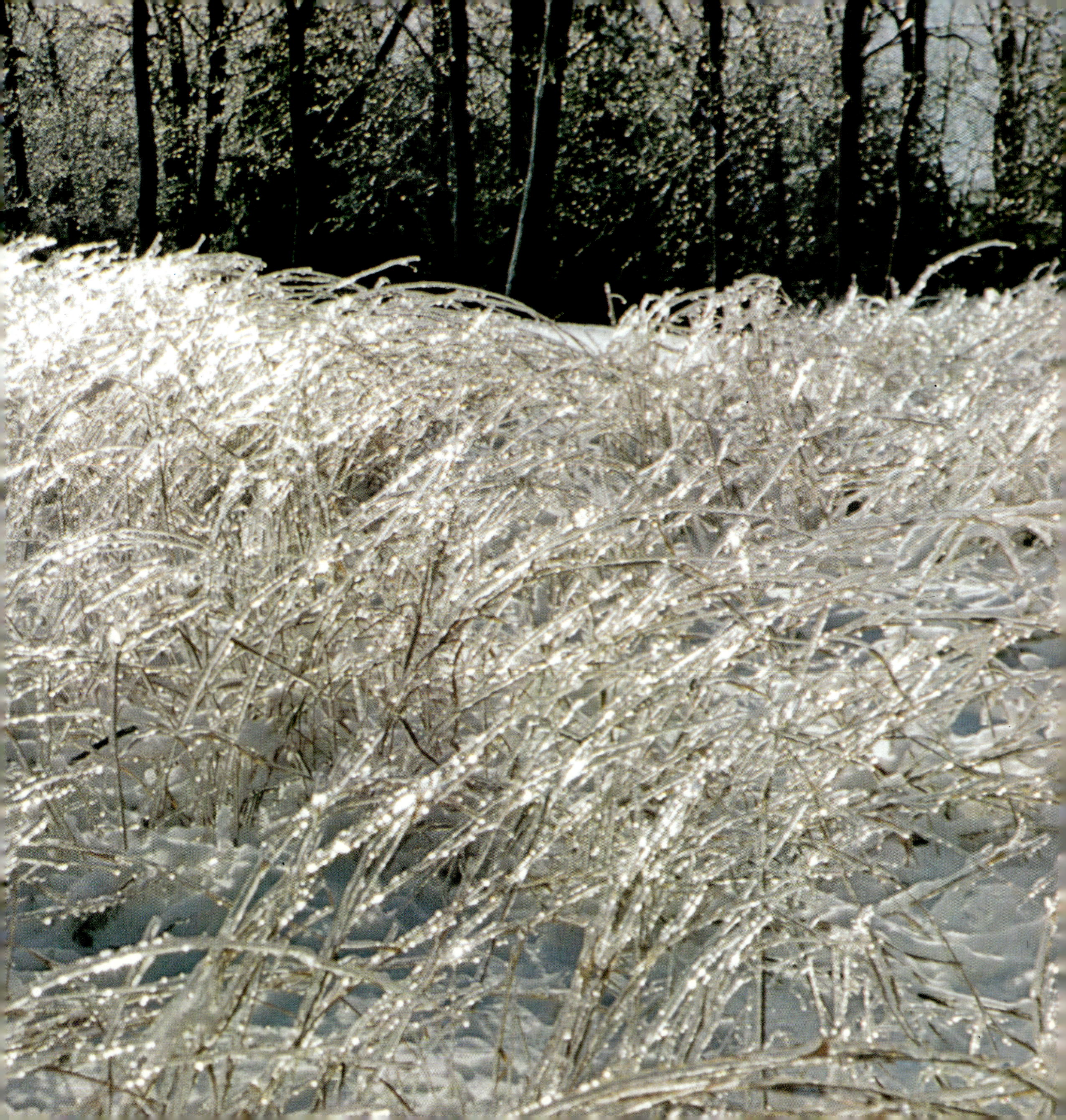

45

White Mountains, New Hampshire.
Ellis River.
June 1973

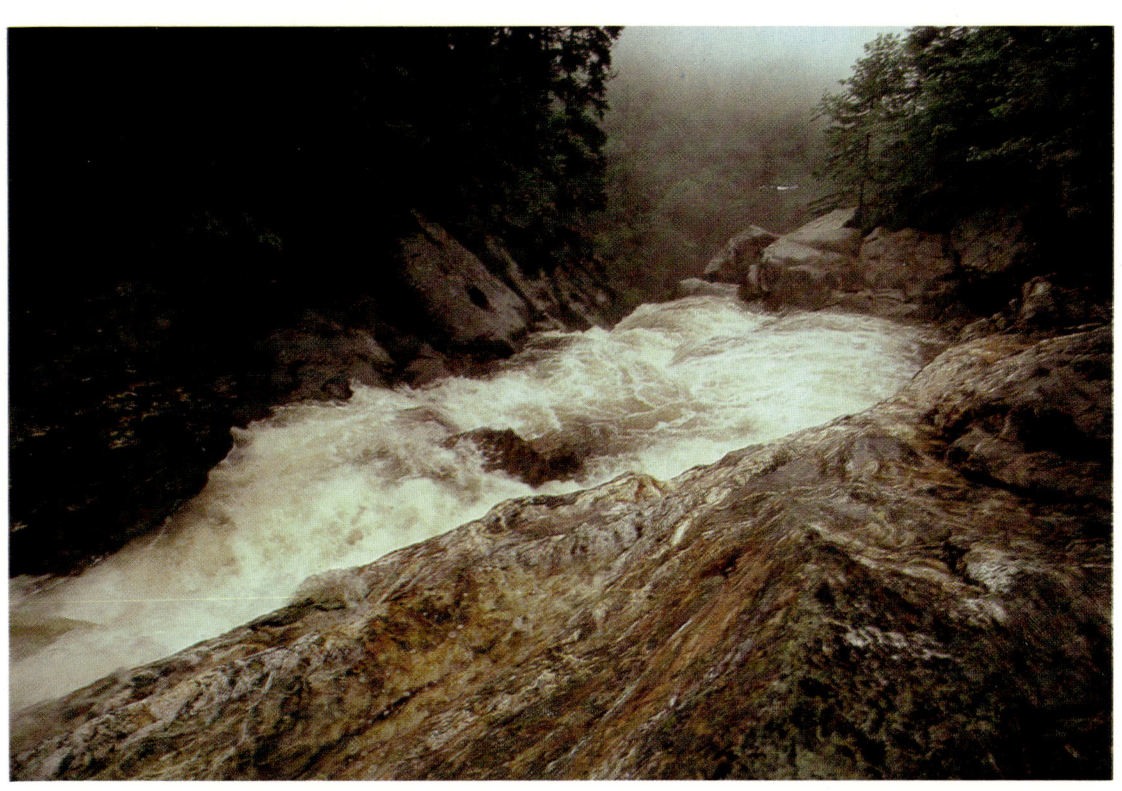

46
White Mountains, New Hampshire.
Zealand Falls.
July 1973

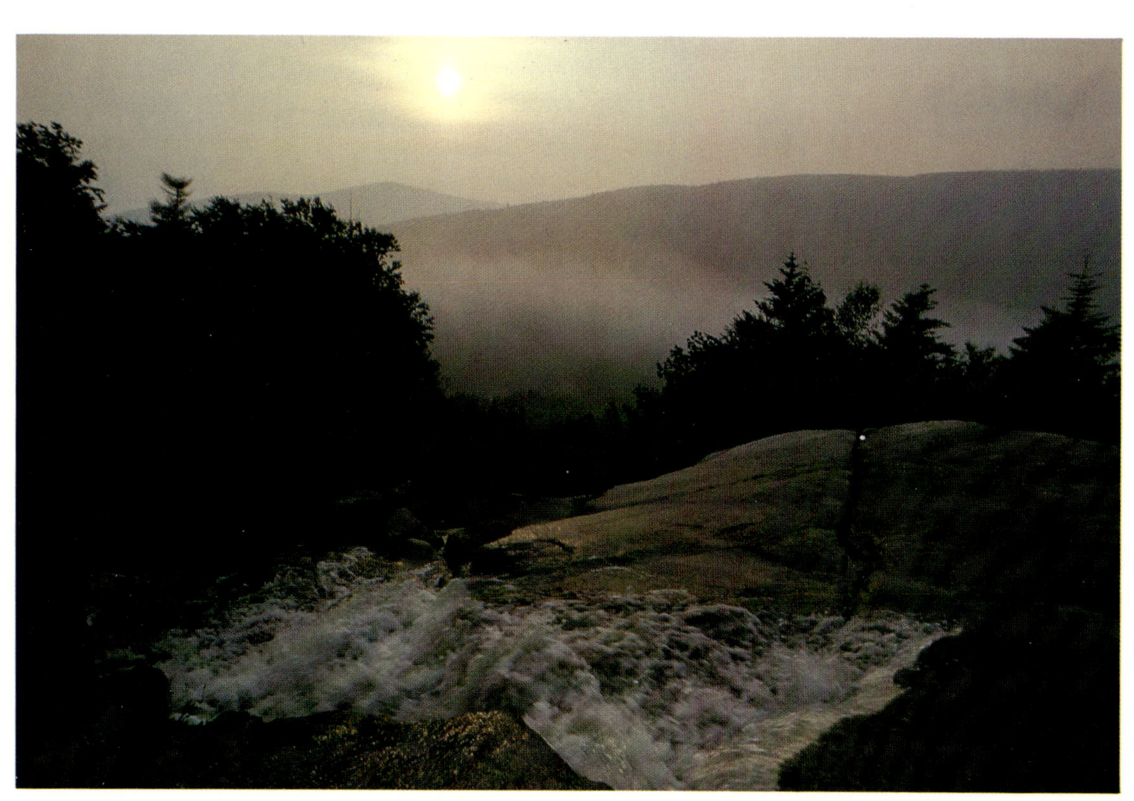

47

White Mountains, New Hampshire.

Table Mountain.

July 5, 1973

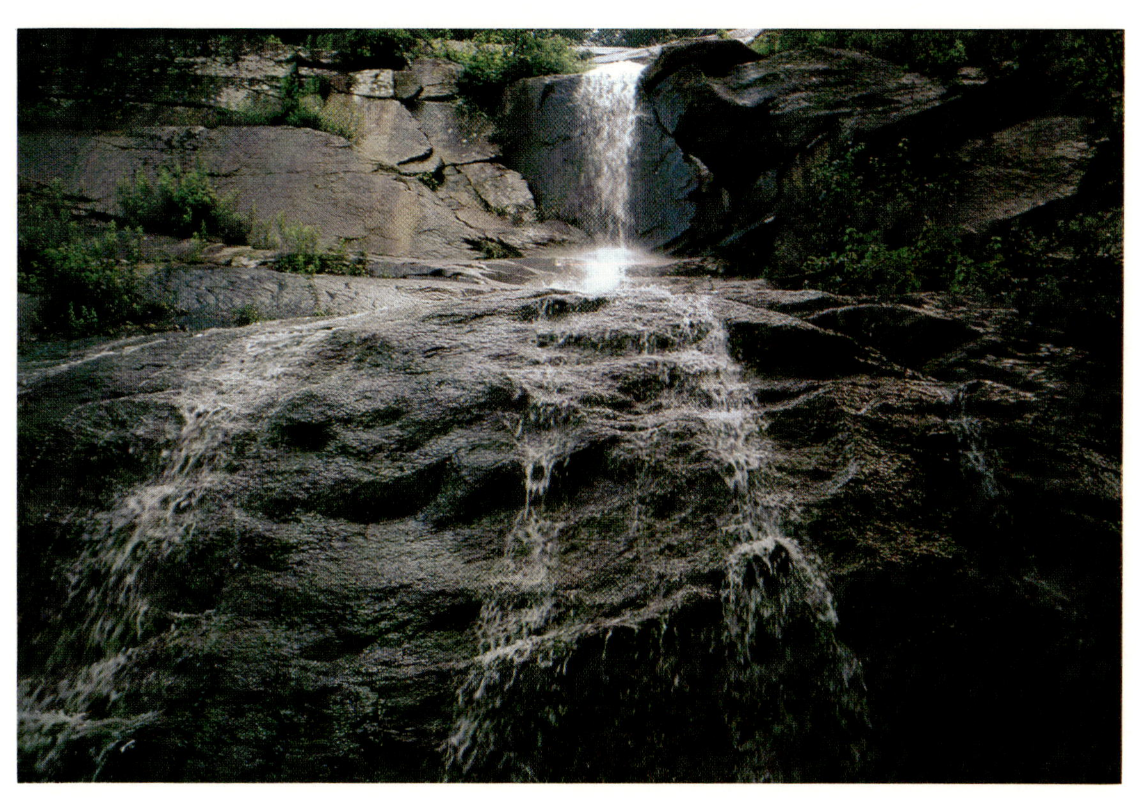

48

White Mountains, New Hampshire.
Table Mountain. The last picture.
July 5, 1973

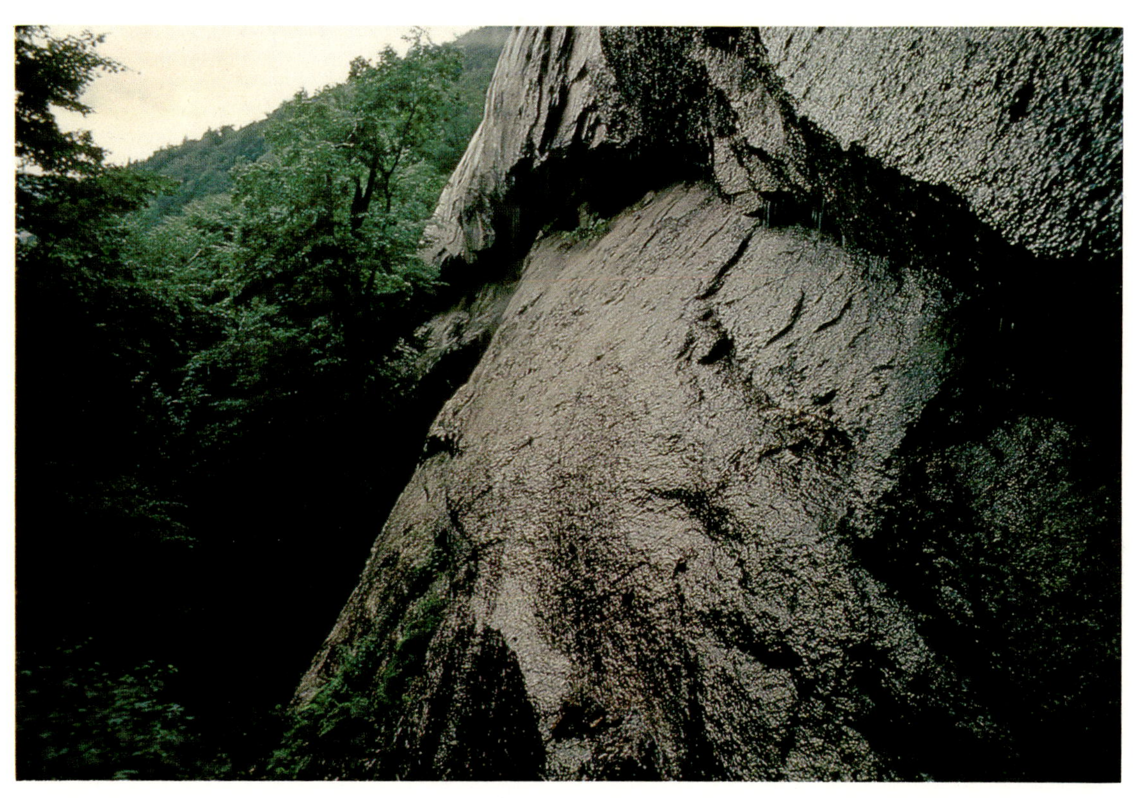